# How to Grow A WINNING QUARTERBACK

Front cover football image and back cover photography provided by Corbis Images.
Front cover photos of Drew Bledsoe and Peyton Manning provided by the NFLCA.
Black and white photography, excluding DVD grabs provided by Keith Hadley.

Published by Cool Springs Press, a Division of Thomas Nelson, Inc.,
P.O. Box 141000, Nashville, Tennessee, 37214

**Library of Congress Cataloging-in-Publication Data is available.**
ISBN 1-930604-97-1

First printing 2003
Printed in the United States of America
10 9 8 7 6 5 4 3 2 1

**Editor:** Ramona D. Wilkes
**Copyeditor:** Jason Zasky
**Proofing:** Sally Graham
**Production/Design:** Joey McNair of Defy Creative

Visit the Thomas Nelson website at www.ThomasNelson.com

The National Football League Coaches Association Presents

# How to Grow
# A WINNING
# QUARTERBACK

## FOR BOYS AGES 8 TO 18

## JERRY RHOME

COOL
SPRINGS
PRESS

Nashville, Tennessee
A Division of Thomas Nelson, Inc.
www.ThomasNelson.com

# Contents

# Foreword

**O**n behalf of the National Football League Coaches Association (NFLCA), I am proud to present this book to young athletes across America. It's one of many projects undertaken by the NFLCA that provide tomorrow's high school, and perhaps even college players, with proven fundamentals that work on the field and off, in the classroom and at home.

The NFLCA was founded in 1996 primarily to assist retired NFL coaches with issues such as salary, insurance, pensions, and other benefits. But the educational and instructional aspect of our work has blossomed in recent years. To date, we have published three instructional books for youths. Our coaches participate in innumerable clinics for junior level, high school and college coaches, and we have produced three highly regarded instructional videotapes that will share NFL coaches' insights with youth, high school, and college coaches around the country.

These tools are just the early fruits of the NFLCA's commitment to educating young football players, their parents, and their coaches. As coaches we know that from quality instruction comes quality play. From quality play comes enjoyment, elevated self-worth, and confidence. We see it in the eyes of the young men we coach every day. With this and the increasingly broad line of NFLCA products and services now available, we're certain that we'll being seeing that look in the eyes of more happily determined kids for years to come.

Larry Kennan
Executive Director
National Football League Coaches Association
Washington, DC

# Introduction

I consider the fact that I was able to play quarterback and make my living coaching in the NFL as two of the great good fortunes of my life. I was extremely lucky because my father was a football coach, and I received expert instruction in the art of playing quarterback from the time I could hold a ball.

As a coach, I have tried to share that lifelong knowledge with the hundreds of young men I have worked with over the last 30 years. As fulfilling as that work has been, I have only been able to personally reach a very small percentage of the youngsters who want to learn about quarterbacking. Ironically, most of the quarterbacks I did reach were young men who had already amassed significant skills.

As the title implies, this book is written specifically for the young quarterback (ages 8 to 18) who is thinking about taking up the position or would simply like to learn more about the game and the role of its most visible player. The book focuses on the basic fundamentals such as those required to take a snap from center, hand off, grip a ball, protect the ball, and pass proficiently. Furthermore, it addresses the mental and emotional side of quarterbacking, including the importance of leadership, dedication and respect for coaches and teammates. Woven throughout the text are examples taken from my personal playing experience both in college and in the NFL, as well as specific examples and case studies of young men I've coached at the highest levels of the game. I include many of the same drills I employed as an NFL coach working with roughly a dozen quarterbacks who played in either the Super Bowl, the Pro Bowl, or both.

In the back of the book, you'll also find a **unique DVD** featuring NFL greats Peyton Manning and Drew Bledsoe. In footage exclusive to this book, these future Hall-of-Famers walk you through how to play quarterback.

My hope for this book/DVD is that it will prepare those who know they want to be a quarterback and educate those who are considering it. In either case, I think it's an ideal first step. I'm proud to share it with you.

Jerry Rhome
Atlanta, Georgia

# ChapterOne

# Handling the Ball

## Are You Mr. Sloppy?

**A**re you sloppy? Be honest. Are you one of those kids whose room is a mess—clothes everywhere, bed unmade, toothbrush out of its holder? It may seem like neatness has nothing to do with playing quarterback, but in reality it has everything to do with it. If you're neat and orderly in your daily life you're more likely to be orderly at practice and on the field. Believe me, if you're going to play quarterback successfully, you need to be especially *organized*.

The quarterback is at the core of virtually every offensive play. If he's organized, the entire offense is likely to run more smoothly.

Why does a quarterback need to be organized? There are several reasons. First, the quarterback is the heart of a football team. The coaching staff is the most important voice on any football team, but the quarterback

is often the team leader. Why? Because he's at the core of every play. Other than the center, the quarterback is the only guy who touches the ball on virtually every play from scrimmage. He's also the link between the coaching staff and the rest of the team. He's the guy who can pick a team up and move it down the field. If he's organized the team will be organized.

Second, a good quarterback—a good team leader—needs to know not only his assignment on each play but also the assignments of nearly all his teammates. As **Peyton Manning** says in the attached DVD, the quarterback is responsible for the other ten players on the offense. Think about it: If a quarterback is supposed to throw a pass on a certain play, wouldn't it help if he knew what his receivers should be doing? Shouldn't he also know where his pass protection will be?

The only way to keep all this stuff in your head is to be organized, and the best way to become organized is to start with your everyday life. Begin with little things like writing down your homework assignments, keeping your bed made, and doing your household chores on a schedule. You'll be amazed at how off-the-field organization will make its way into your life as a quarterback. Before you know it, you'll be showing up at practice a little early. You'll start to show consistency. The player who takes the time to make sure his toothbrush is in its holder will soon take note of on-the-field details. I've seen a lot of guys who

wasted talent by being sloppy both on and off the field. Once they realized that sloppiness can really drag down a quarterback's performance, they straightened up. I've seen that newfound sense of organization turn careers around.

## The Exchange

There is no better place to begin achieving on-field consistency than the center-quarterback exchange. The key to a successful exchange is mutual trust and understanding. The quarter-back and center must know that the exchange will be done the same way every snap, every practice, every game, every day. That trust is accomplished through repetition and practicing the correct fundamentals.

First, stand up at the line of scrimmage. As a quarterback, always strive for good posture. Don't let yourself get all hunched down so you have to look through the top of your helmet to see what's in front of you.

Next, when placing your hands in position to accept the snap from center, you must put them in the same spot—in the same position relative to one another, with the same pressure on the center's tail—on every play. When I was play-ing, the very first thing I would do is place my throwing hand under the center's rump and press a little with the back of my hand just so he would know where I was. That way I didn't have to worry about getting the ball, and the center could concern himself with his own

**The Snap**

**Track 3**

assignment instead of worrying about where my hands were.

**It's critical that your hands be not only in the right place but also in the right formation to accept the snap. Join your hands by placing the two thumbs touching, side-by-side, extended to their full length. For a right-handed player the right hand will be on top, the opposite for a left-hander. The lower hand should be slightly behind and slightly off to the side (to the left for a right-hander and vice versa). When the ball is snapped, it should hit the quarterback's top hand first. The quarterback then brings his bottom hand under the ball to secure it.**

The most common mistake with the

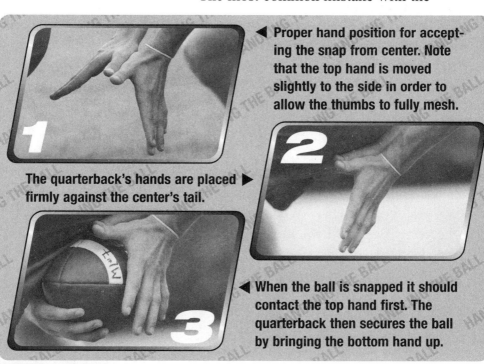

◀ Proper hand position for accepting the snap from center. Note that the top hand is moved slightly to the side in order to allow the thumbs to fully mesh.

The quarterback's hands are placed ▶ firmly against the center's tail.

◀ When the ball is snapped it should contact the top hand first. The quarterback then secures the ball by bringing the bottom hand up.

exchange occurs when the quarterback gets sloppy and inattentive to detail. Instead of making sure his hands are in the correct position on *every* play, on one play he puts his hands a little to the side or a little too low or too high. The center misses the quarterback's hands, and the result is a fumble.

Another common mistake is that the quarterback does not extend his fingers in the ready position, and when the ball comes back, instead of hitting the quarterback's palm it hits a finger. That not only hurts, but it can cause a fumble as well.

Finally, it's important that from the moment you put your hands beneath the center, you are ready to receive a snap. Even though the snap count may be on 3, a smart, alert quarterback plans for the unexpected, such as a center snapping the ball on the wrong count or snapping the ball early for some other reason. If you're behind center and you're not ready, you're looking at a possible turnover or broken finger.

## TIPS

- Be organized on and off the field
- Strive for good posture and a balanced stance
- Extend your fingers for the snap

# Moving Away from Center

Once the center has snapped the ball and the offensive line is exploding off the line of scrimmage, it's time for you to enter the next phase of the play. But it's important to remember that you can't go anywhere without the ball. In other words, make sure you have a secure grip on the football *with both hands* before you even think about pulling away from the center and handing off, running, passing, or pitching the football.

How do you make sure you have a secure grip on the ball? Many coaches teach their quarterbacks to "follow the center." In other words, they want the quarterback's hands to move with the center's butt for a brief moment during the snap. Be careful not to overdo this. Personally, I have never felt comfortable telling quarterbacks to do this because on most plays as soon as the ball is snapped the center should be moving in one direction and the quarterback in another. I feel that if your hand is pressed snugly up against the center and your hands are in the proper formation, you'll get the ball cleanly and shouldn't have to consciously think about following the center.

Now you've got the ball, and the play calls for you to fake a hand-off, pitch the ball, drop back, or roll out. No matter what you're going to do next, the very first thing you do now is "stomach" the ball. **Once the ball leaves the**

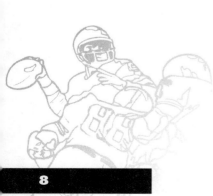

**center's hands, the very first place it should go is right to your stomach with two hands— one on each side of the ball.**

Every play a quarterback makes starts with good ball handling and ball protection technique (we'll discuss ball protection later on). Let's start with the basic hand-off technique.

Handing off is not usually a quarterback's favorite thing to do. Most young quarterbacks would much rather pass the ball, run it, or pitch it than simply hand it off and watch someone else run. Because most quarterbacks don't like to do it, many of them do it carelessly. But if you ever hope to play quarterback in high school or college, you need to do everything well, not just your favorite parts of the job.

**Joe Theismann**, whom I coached with the Washington Redskins, had a great reputation as a passer and was a great quarterback. But one of the things that made Joe so successful at Notre Dame and in the NFL was that he always took great pride in his ball handling. More recently, I would point to **John Elway** as a great ball handler, and from today's crop of NFL players it's hard to beat Peyton Manning. As you'll see in the enclosed DVD, Peyton himself says, "A lot of quarterbacks just want to practice passing, but you need to practice snaps, hand-offs, and pitches as well."

The first key to a good hand-off is for the quarterback to understand that it's his job to get the ball to the runner, not vice versa. A runner's job is to get to the hole. The quarterback must

The Hand-off

**Track 4**

**DVD Review**

In a hand-off, the ball should be delivered with authority into the runner's belly.

get him the ball in time to hit the hole, without the runner having to slow down.

In a hand-off, the ball should start in the safety of the quarterback's stomach, held securely by two hands. The quarterback then takes the footsteps laid out by his coach for that particular play. **With both hands, he places the ball into the stomach of the ball carrier. The ball is not slid in across the runner's gut, it's popped in. In other words, as the quarterback places the ball in the runner's belly he gives it a little emphasis—boom!— right in the navel.** This way the ball carrier never has to worry about where the football is. Once the quarterback has signed off with that "pop," he smoothly slides his hand out of the runner's belly and moves away.

**One often overlooked key to successful hand-offs is the eyes. On every single hand-off, even fake hand-offs (which we'll address next), the eyes of the quarterback should be looking right into the spot on the runner's belly where he intends to put the ball.** Pretend there is a bulls-eye right around the runner's navel. As a player and as a coach I've always likened the quarterback to a matador who's keeping his eye on a charging bull. I tell my quarterbacks—be real smooth with your feet and real smooth with your hands as the ball carrier goes by.

If you watch quarterbacks at the high school, college, or even pro level, you'll sometimes see the quarterback "ride" the ball carri-

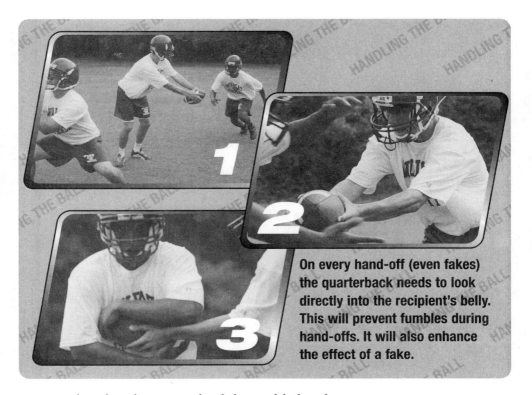

On every hand-off (even fakes) the quarterback needs to look directly into the recipient's belly. This will prevent fumbles during hand-offs. It will also enhance the effect of a fake.

er, meaning that the quarterback keeps his hand in the runner's belly for a brief period of time as the runner heads for the hole. This should only happen on certain plays. If you're running a play that calls for a straight hand-off, the ball just goes in, there's a slight "pop" and the hands are removed. You don't want to keep your hands in there because you risk dragging the ball out. Now, if you're talking about faking, there is a time when your hands are in there and you pull the ball out. We'll get to that in a minute.

**TIPS**

- ■ Master the hand-off
- ■ "POP" the football into the ball carrier's belly
- ■ See the ball into his navel

After the quarterback makes the hand-off and the ball is secured in the runner's belly, is the quarterback's job finished? No. He may have to go and fake to another back. The play may call for him to fake a pass or continue in another direction as if he still has the ball. So, once the ball is handed off, the quarterback's hands should go right back to his own stomach, and he should continue as if he still has the ball. Why? Because you never know who's watching. You should continue your fake, as you may have someone on the other team or on the opposing sideline who's got his eyes on you. The more you can keep them guessing about what you're doing the better. If you hand the ball off and automatically drop your hands, relax your body, and become a spectator, you're letting everybody know that the runner has the ball. If you can trick just one guy on any given play, that might be the difference between scoring a touchdown and not scoring. Remember, you never know who's watching.

## *Faking*

Two of the best fakers I ever coached were **Doug Williams** and **Chris Chandler**. I used to call Williams "The Magician" because he did a great job every time he faked. Neither one of these guys came to it naturally, either. They improved because they committed to being good at it, were conscientious, and took pride in it.

There are three basic ways to fake a hand-off. **In the *blank hand* fake, you start with your two hands on the ball and the ball "stomached" safely in your own gut. As you step toward the decoy runner your lead hand (the one nearest the line of scrimmage) goes into his stomach. Meanwhile the other hand has the ball buried in your own stomach so it's secure. The blank hand goes into the runner's stomach, the same spot, the same way that you would on a real hand-off, and then it comes back out.** This kind of fake is especially common in offenses that feature two or three backs in the backfield.

Now, the play may call for the quarterback to make one fake and then hand off to another runner. In this instance, the lead hand would fake to the first back, come out, and then join with the other hand to briefly stomach the ball. Then you would take the ball and pop it into the ball carrier's belly.

The *bootleg* fake has the quarterback faking a hand-off and running around the end. **The bootleg calls for the quarterback to secure the**

**Play Action Fake**

**Track 18**

**ball not with two hands in his stomach, but with one hand against his back hip, concealing it from defenders.**

There's a third fake that's a little trickier called a *belly fake*. We talked about it earlier. **That's where the quarterback actually places the ball into a runner's belly for a split second with the option of taking the ball back out or leaving it with the runner. The key here is that both the quarterback and the runner be clear that the runner is not to automatically take the ball but that he is to cover it loosely with his arms and allow the quarterback to make the decision to give or go**. Your coach will tell you how to make that decision.

The key to good faking is obvious: If every play—fake or actual hand-off—has the quarterback doing the exact same thing, the defense will never be able to tell fakes from the real thing. Unfortunately, a sloppy player doesn't do that. Instead of really following through—acting as though he has the ball even on hand-offs—he gets lazy. He eases up his body as soon as the ball carrier gets past him. After a little bit of that, the defense knows how to read the quarterback and realizes much more quickly who does and who doesn't have the ball. So always carry out your fake.

Some kids like to add a certain sense of exaggeration to their fakes. While I appreciate the intent, I don't really like exaggerated fakes. I think it's a common sense thing. What would

The bootleg is a more elaborate fake, but the quarterback still needs to look directly into the running back's belly.

fool a defender more, having the quarterback do the same thing at the end of every play or, after a fake, doing gyrations as if he's got the ball? I think everything should look alike, and that's what I try to get across to young quarterbacks. Make it all look alike. You have to be a little bit of an actor as a quarterback. And if you're really going to be good, you have to act out your part. Watch how Peyton Manning "sets the hook" for a fake in the DVD.

## Pitching

One of the best pitching offenses that I was ever involved in was with the Cleveland Browns. I didn't have the privilege of having **Jim Brown** as a teammate (he had retired prior to my arrival in Cleveland), but after his retirement we continued to run the pitch play that was his favorite. When I got there, I executed it with the man who replaced Brown, the great **Leroy Kelley**. The legendary coach **Blanton Collier** taught me how to do this play. He was the head coach, and he had been Jim Brown's backfield coach.

Leroy was really, really quick out of the blocks, and my assignment was to take a little shuffle step and then pitch the ball from my stomach with two hands, very similar to a chest pass in basketball. I would open up towards Leroy, shuffle, and then flip the ball with my arms extended. The ball basically traveled like a knuckleball, but it would get there quickly

The Toss

Track 6

and accurately. I've taught that pitch to some guys in pro ball, and some of them have liked it and others have laughed. I'd say "Listen, if it's good enough for Jim Brown it ought to be good enough for us."

The key to any good pitch is control. You need to know where your target is, and you need to be under control at the time of the pitch. You also need to control the trajectory. I see a lot of young quarterbacks who "sling" the ball. They take the snap from center, their arms are extended, and then they throw a slinging underneath pitch that is very hard to control. When you sling the ball you risk inconsistency. Sometimes you'll hang on too long, sometimes you let it go too fast. Either way, the resulting pitch is often sloppy, causing a fumble. That's why I've always coached my players—in high school, college, and the NFL—to stomach the ball before doing anything else with it. Young quarterbacks just want to take it and throw it out there. If you do, you're going to get unpredictable results.

Now the other kind of pitch—one that's used for longer tosses—is the one-handed pitch. One hand just rotates the ball and basically passes it underhanded—a lateral. The idea is to put a spiral in the ball so it will travel a little farther and cover that ground accurately. This pitch still starts with two hands.

Obviously pitches are made with the hands and arms. But the most often overlooked key to good pitching is body position and

footwork/legwork. **In order to be accurate, you need to have your knees bent, and you ought to be in a slightly bent, athletic position. You need to be balanced, with your feet underneath your body, not in front of you or behind you. Don't be overextended. Be under control**. Basically you shuffle your feet towards the target and follow through.

The pitch itself is all about timing. I've worked with young quarterbacks who struggle with pitching and almost inevitably their problem is footwork and timing. **You need to step as you pitch.** There's a little bit of a rhythm to it.

## The Option Pitch

The option pitch is totally different. **In the option, you are moving down the line of scrimmage towards a certain defensive player. You have the ball chest-high—held securely in two hands. When you are confronted with a defensive player, you have to make a decision on whether to fake a pitch and run the ball, or pitch it to a teammate. Your coach can help you understand which decision to make.**

**The pitch itself starts with two hands. Then the ball is grasped by the hand closest to the intended ball carrier. The next step is a little flipping motion in which your palm turns out toward the ball carrier, your fingers extend to propel the ball, and your thumb rotates from the top half of the ball to the bottom half. As the ball leaves your hand,**

**The Option**

**Track 7**

**your thumb should be pointing at the ground between you and the ball carrier.**

The eyes are very important on all pitches, and in the option it's particularly difficult to look at your target because you're running at the defensive end or linebacker, and basically you're looking him straight in the eye, trying to figure out whether he's playing you or the pitch. It's only out of the corner of your eye, using your peripheral vision, that you're seeing the potential ball carrier. It's something that you really have to practice often. That practice will build confidence.

DVD Review

Peyton Manning demonstrates the option pitch.

**As you get ready to pitch the ball, don't crouch too low, but don't stand too tall either, otherwise you'll be giving the defensive end a bigger target to hit**. As for the hit—and it will come—you've got to learn to give with the blow. As you pitch you've got to relax a little bit. Expect the hit but relax your body as much as possible. This will help you absorb the impact. This same advice holds true for throwing the ball under pressure. Just relax and go with the blow.

From time to time on a running play or a pass play, something will go wrong. Maybe a running back will head in the wrong direction and won't be in place to take a pitch. Maybe a defensive lineman will break through the line and make it impossible (or too risky) to attempt a pitch. On such broken plays the quarterback needs to make a quick decision. As Peyton Manning says on the DVD, it's situations like

this where a quarterback's knowledge of the play pays off. "If you really understand the play—you know the blocking scheme—go ahead and get to the hole," he says.

## TIPS

- Play out your fakes
- Stomach the ball on pitch plays
- Be under control for the pitch
- Key on the defensive player, make him commit
- Use your peripheral vision
- Expect/absorb the hit

## Drills

One note about the drills sections that follow throughout this book: Every football coach has his favorite drills. Some of them are very simple, and some are very complex. I tend to prefer simple drills. In fact, I think some of the most effective drills a young player can do are the kind he can invent at home and do alone or with a buddy or two. The key for you as an aspiring quarterback is to use your imagination to sharpen your game at home, during downtime, and throughout the off-season.

## ✓1. Dexterity Drill

One drill that I used a lot in the NFL is flipping a basketball around among the quarterbacks. A basketball is considerably larger than a football, and after working with the larger ball a football just seems that much easier to handle.

## ✓2. Center Exchange Drill

This is a light drill that young football players can organize on their own. **Line up the centers in a line and place a quarterback behind each center.** One of the quarterbacks starts the cadence, and the other quarterbacks join in. After three snaps, the quarterbacks rotate to the next center, call signals, take two or three snaps, and move down the line. This helps in two ways. First, each quarterback becomes familiar with each center and vice versa. Second, by calling the signals together the quarterbacks will eventually adopt the same cadence, reducing the problems that arise when a substitute quarterback enters the game. I liked to run this drill every day for 5 or 10 minutes prior to practice, but quarterbacks and centers can get together on their own and do it over the summer. It helps with the most important foundation to any play—a successful quarterback-center

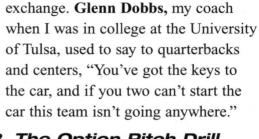

exchange. **Glenn Dobbs,** my coach when I was in college at the University of Tulsa, used to say to quarterbacks and centers, "You've got the keys to the car, and if you two can't start the car this team isn't going anywhere."

### ✓ 3. The Option Pitch Drill

One of the reasons that so few teams run the option is the amount of time it takes to perfect it in practice. I've played on and coached option teams, and we spent boatloads of time practicing and drilling the option. **You can practice it too. Put a blocking dummy out on the field or even pick a lone tree in your yard. That becomes the defensive end. You, the quarterback, come down the imaginary line of scrimmage and pitch the ball to your buddy or even another tree or a garbage can.** The option is tough for young kids. The more you practice it and the more you drill it, the better you become at it. See how often you can hit your target with the pitched ball using only your peripheral vision.

# ChapterTwo

# Protecting the Ball

## Don't Be a Give-It-Up Quarterback

I f you watch much football on television, you hear coaches and broadcasters talking about the importance of limiting turnovers. That's because the surest way to lose a game is to give up more fumbles or interceptions than your opponent. If you don't believe that, look at the 2001 NFL season. The teams with the worst turnover ratios in the NFL were the Detroit Lions and the Minnesota Vikings. Combined, those two teams won just seven games.

The goal of an offense is to score points, but the only way you're going to do that is by protecting the ball. That's why the first step we talked about in the last chapter was stomaching the ball for security. Once the play gets going you always have to be conscious of the ball as well. After a play starts, anything can happen. You don't know when you're going to be hit from the side. You may even be knocked over by your own teammate. Let's say the ball carrier doesn't take the right steps—Bam! There are many ball carriers or pulling guards that have run over a quarterback.

In football, the biggest threat is not always the opposing middle linebacker or a fierce defensive end—sometimes it's a team's own quarterback. A quarterback can beat his own team if he doesn't protect the ball. A quarterback can throw three touchdown passes, but if he turns the ball over to

the defense four times there's a good chance you're going to lose, just because the quarterback failed to protect the football.

The concept of protecting the ball is even more important today than it was when I was playing football. The aggressiveness with which defenses now try to steal the ball from ball carriers has increased dramatically. It's become a big thing. NFL defenses have done drills for the last 20 years in which they have guys run alongside ball carriers and try to slap the ball out. Defensive coaches are teaching these techniques, and you see it happen in games far more than you did 20 years ago. These days a good quarterback not only has to have offensive skills, he needs to think like a defensive player and know where and when he might be vulnerable to attack.

## Protecting the Ball in Bad Weather

Cold and/or wet weather is one of the biggest contributing factors in turnovers. Obviously, the worse the weather the more you have to pay attention to all details, particularly the protection of the ball. The first thing to focus on is making sure you get the snap from center securely in your hands before you think about anything else. If you can't get the ball snapped safely, you're dead. You're probably going to lose at least half of those fumbles. In real bad weather, think like the driver of a car—slow

down and be even more deliberate than usual. Make sure that the center is feeling you and don't be too anxious to pull your hands away once you get the ball. Make sure you're getting the ball securely before you move away from the center.

## *Passing in the Pocket*

Protecting the ball while passing in the pocket is the same thing. At the precise moment that a quarterback is getting ready to throw the ball, that's when he is most vulnerable. At that point there's a decision to be made with regard to protecting the ball or advancing it. A good pocket quarterback can feel that pressure and assess the various risks. It's vital that when you're in the pocket, you're thinking not only about receivers' routes but also about protecting the ball.

**The thing that I'm appalled by—and I see it all the time—is these guys running around with the ball in one hand sticking out from their body. When I was coaching we used to say a guy was carrying the ball "like a loaf of bread." A good quarterback—a smart quarterback—keeps the ball tucked until he's good and ready to either pass, hand-off, pitch, or fake.**

I've had a couple of quarterbacks that were absolute butterfingers; they had the worst reputation for fumbling the ball, even at the NFL level. That's primarily because they grew up

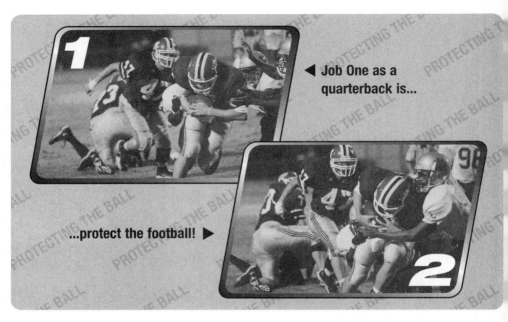

◀ Job One as a quarterback is...

...protect the football! ▶

being sloppy and got away with it. Maybe as youngsters they had such strong arms that no one really confronted them about protecting the ball. But as you move up the ranks from high school to college and to the pros, scouts look for those kinds of things to give their team an advantage. The scouting reports might say, "This guy is a fumbler, go after the ball."

It all starts when you're a little kid learning how to protect the football. I always say to a young quarterback: When you're getting hit— when you know you're going to be tackled, or if you're trying to escape—tuck the ball away into your stomach and protect it with everything you've got.

When you're throwing on the run it's the same thing. You've got the ball out and you're trying to throw. If someone comes along and begins to tackle you or pull you down, tuck the ball away. If you try to be a hero, either by breaking away or throwing a last minute pass, odds are you're going to fumble, throw an interception, or get hurt. So as a youngster you've got to make a habit of protecting the ball. Don't take chances. A little bit of a loss in yardage is a whole lot better than a turnover. And you don't want to gain a reputation as a fumbler. Don't get me wrong. If you can escape safely, do it, but be careful. Making smart decisions while gambling is one of the hallmarks of a winning quarterback.

## *Running With The Ball*

Every player who touches the ball in the course of a game has to protect it. Just because you're a quarterback doesn't give you an excuse.

Quarterbacks fumble just like anybody else. So, when you are running with the ball put it away. Put it away just like a halfback or a wide receiver does.

Note that in both this ▶ photo and the previous images, the runners are carrying the ball correctly, that is tucked in close to their bodies and in the arm farthest from tacklers.

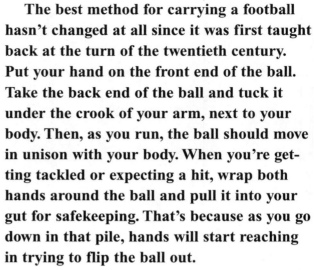

The best method for carrying a football hasn't changed at all since it was first taught back at the turn of the twentieth century. Put your hand on the front end of the ball. Take the back end of the ball and tuck it under the crook of your arm, next to your body. Then, as you run, the ball should move in unison with your body. When you're getting tackled or expecting a hit, wrap both hands around the ball and pull it into your gut for safekeeping. That's because as you go down in that pile, hands will start reaching in trying to flip the ball out.

Next, you should always run with the ball facing away from the nearest threat. If a tackler or tacklers are approaching you from your right side, the ball should be on your left. If they're approaching from the left, the ball should be on your right. You want to make sure that the ball is on your upfield side, the side furthest from likely contact.

Finally, once you get into open field running, you want to keep the ball protected from oncoming tacklers. So if a tackler is approaching you from your left, slide the ball into your right hand grip and vice versa. One important note about protecting the ball while running: Never try to change ball position while you're in the midst of contact or in heavy traffic.

**TIPS** ◄ ▬ ▬ ▬ ▬ ▬ ▬ ▬ ▬ ▬ ▬ ▬ ▬ ▬

- Turnovers lose games
- Expect the unexpected hit
- Slow down, grip the ball loosely in bad weather
- Tuck the ball away when running

## Drills

### ✓1. Bad-Weather Drill

One of the bad-weather drills I used to do, even in the NFL, was to place a football in a bucket of water and have the quarterback and center get used to working with the slippery leather. Former head coach **Jim Hanifan** loved that drill. I coached with him in St. Louis, and one day he came walking out to the practice field with two big buckets. I asked him, "What are you going to do?" He said, "We're going to practice snapping the ball in the rain."

If you're going to use this drill you better use old balls or make sure you can afford to get a few new ones, but it's a great way to get ready for foul weather.

### ✓2. Fumble-Proofing Drill

When I was coaching, I'd line up a tunnel of

The gauntlet is a time-honored drill for preventing fumbles. I line up 6 or 7 guys on either side of a ball carrier and have him try to run through the lane while they try to pull the ball out.

guys—half a dozen or so on one side and same on the other. We'd give the quarterback the ball and have him run through the gauntlet while each defender reached in and tried to pull the football out of his hand. I'd also have the passer go back with a couple of guys rushing him and trying to knock the ball out of his hand. The quarterbacks would react by protecting the ball and scrambling out of the pocket. I would always make sure the quarterback put the ball away and scrambled out rather than just taking off with the ball swinging wildly. This is something you can keep in mind even in your backyard pickup games.

# ChapterThree

# Passing vs. Throwing

## Arm Strength and Accuracy

**W**hat's the difference between throwing a rock and passing a football? Everything. Early in my career, when I was the quarterbacks coach for the Seattle Seahawks, we had a tryout camp, and there was a young man

**Arm Strength & Accuracy**

**Track 12**

there who had an absolute rocket launcher for an arm. This guy was so strong he could throw the ball through a wall. We signed him but ended up letting him go before training camp because he threw rocks. He could *throw* the ball as far as you could ever want, but he couldn't *pass* it.

Throwing is about power; passing is about *power, accuracy, touch,* and *timing.* When you throw a rock you just go back and throw it. But in passing a football there are all kinds of things that have to go through your mind: Where are you going to place the ball? How hard are you gonna pass it? Are you going to put loft on it? Are you going to put touch on it? Is it a type of pass that you throw as hard as you can or a pass that you throw softly because of the distance you are from the receiver? There's also a certain amount that you have to lead the receiver. How fast is he running and where is the defender?

A quarterback is not unlike a conductor. When a conductor is directing the symphony he has to know what every single instrument is doing, and he has to anticipate the next note. A conductor may look like he's just swinging his baton, but each move means something. In football, fans watch a quarterback pass the football and think he's just throwing it. But each pass is different, and the way he passes the ball on each play is going to make a difference in whether it's complete or not. When you're throwing a rock into a pond, there are no risks. The great Ohio State coach **Woody Hayes** used to say, "In passing there are three possible outcomes, and two of them—interceptions and incompletions—are bad."

If you play quarterback long enough you will come up against rock throwers. Everybody will be excited about the rock thrower because he can throw it so far and so hard. The only problem is that he rarely hits his receivers, and when he does, few of them can catch it. Then the passer comes along. When he *passes* the ball it always seems to be an easy catch. In fact, if you look at the great receivers of all time you'll almost always find a great quarterback who got him the ball in the right place at the right time with the right speed and the right touch. **Steve Largent** may be the best football player I've ever seen. This is partially because of the great quarterbacks he played with, like **Jim Zorn** and **Dave Krieg** in Seattle. The better the receiver the better the passer, and the better the passer the better the receiver, but it all starts with the passer. If he can't put that ball in a position where the receiver can make an easy catch, then you have problems. As **Drew Bledsoe** says in the DVD, "Accuracy beats arm strength every time."

## The Grip

I have no hard and fast rules for gripping a football in preparation for a pass. The number one thing that you're looking for in gripping a football is you want to be comfortable and you want the ball to be balanced in your hand. Some great quarterbacks have held the ball in the middle of it; some great quarterbacks have held the ball entirely on the back third of the ball. Personally, I don't have real large hands. Throughout my career I gripped the ball in such a way that the end of my pinky finger barely reached the laces and my ring finger crossed the laces. For my hand size, that gave me balance on the football. You'll see in the DVD that Drew Bledsoe has very large hands. His index finger reaches almost all the way to the point of the ball while his pinky reaches the laces.

There are three basic rules on grip:
**First, make sure that you're holding the ball where it feels balanced in your hand. Most kids will do this naturally. Because we each have different sized hands our grips may differ.**

**Secondly, use fingertip control. In other**

**The Grip**

**Track 9**

Drew Bledsoe makes a point of leaving daylight between his palm and the football.

words, don't wrap your entire hand—palm and all—around the surface of the ball. Hold it so that only the ends of your fingers are actually making contact with the surface. When you hold the ball up in the air you should be able to see daylight between the ball and the palm of your hand.

Finally, do not squeeze the ball. Too much tension in holding the ball will hinder your ability to handle it and pass it. A nice, firm, controlled grip will always do the trick. Now when you're working with a wet ball grip it even a little looser and really concentrate on fingertip control. The harder you try to grip it in the rain the more likely it's going to slip out

Be careful not to squeeze the ball too tightly when you grip it. Too tight a grip will restrict your throwing motion.

of your hand. As for passing into the wind, most kids think they have to throw harder when the wind is in their face. That's not necessarily true. The key to passing into the wind is to remember that it's not how hard you throw it, it's how accurate your spiral is. It's how tight the spiral is coming out of your hand that dictates the success you'll enjoy on a windy day. It makes sense; a wobbly pass gives the wind a chance to slow the ball down or even knock it off course. A tight spiral bores through the wind, defeating the wind's ability to alter its flight.

Essentially, the grip is up to the player; it's what feels right and what works. I would not change a quarterback's grip unless I was certain that he would throw the ball better by altering it. Take former Cowboys quarterback **Troy Aikman**. He may be the best quarterback I've ever coached in my life. When I first started working with him in Dallas, I tossed him a ball and told him to show me his grip. He wrapped his entire hand around the ball—never even bothered with the laces. It didn't even matter where they were. He just had his hand wrapped around the ball, and his whole hand covered the laces. It was as though he was palming a basketball. But the one thing he did have was daylight; there was daylight between his palm and the ball.

Troy threw as tight a spiral as anybody I've ever seen. Another guy who threw a great spiral was **Warren Moon**. Warren basically had three fingers on the laces, but the tips of his fingers were not on the laces. It was more like the middles of his fingers were on them.

One final note on the grip. Drew makes a great point on the DVD. For real young kids the best way to learn how to grip and throw a football is to use a small ball. NFL- and college-

sized balls are just too big for a lot of 7- to 12-year-olds. As Drew says, learn the fundamentals on a small ball, and by the time your hands are big enough for a larger ball, your technique will be solid. Be patient. Remember, Drew was a backup on his seventh grade team, but he went on to become one of the finest quarterbacks in the NFL.

## TIPS

- Grip should be comfortable and balanced
- Use fingertip control
- Don't squeeze the ball

## The Release

Throughout the history of the game there've been many different kinds of releases. When I was in high school I visited a college where the coach taught all his quarterbacks to keep the ball up above their head when dropping back to pass. When it was time to throw, the ball went up above the ear, and the ball was released high above the head. Needless to say, I decided not to go to that school.

If you look at trading cards from the 1950s and '60s you'll see a lot of those guys have their left arm extended out in front of them and their right hand high above their heads. That's the old-time trading card passing picture. But it's not athletic, and it's certainly not natural.

Before you get too wrapped up in your release, ask yourself the following: How accurately are you passing the ball right now? If you're consistently missing your receivers you may need to focus on your release. Secondly, how quick is the ball coming out of your hand? If your release is too slow the ball will travel slowly, making it easier for a defender to make an interception. How is your trajectory? If for some reason the ball is coming out too low and you're hitting your linemen in the helmet then maybe you need to change your delivery. If you're not having any of these problems you probably don't need to change your release. For those who do need to work on their release, here are some pointers.

The Pass
**Track 10**

Passing a football is not about your arm, it's about your whole body. The pass starts with your toes and ends with your fingers. But the key to releasing the ball lies not in the wrist or the fingers or the elbow, but in the palm of the hand. The palm should turn out. In other words, as you let go of the ball your hand is basically pivoting outward with your thumb swinging around from inside to outside—the opposite of throwing a curve in baseball.

**If you really want to practice a good release you don't even need a ball. Just sit there and flip your hand out. Flip your hand out like you're throwing something out of your hand. Your palm should turn outward and your thumb should come around from inside to outside.**

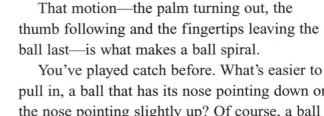

That motion—the palm turning out, the thumb following and the fingertips leaving the ball last—is what makes a ball spiral.

You've played catch before. What's easier to pull in, a ball that has its nose pointing down or the nose pointing slightly up? Of course, a ball pointing up is easier to catch. How can you be sure that your passes are flying nose up? Easy. This drill is demonstrated by coach **Carl Smith** in the DVD. Stand about 8 or 10 feet from a wall and pass the football into the wall. If the nose of the ball is pointing slightly up as it should, the ball will bounce off the wall to the left. See if you can get your passes to do that. (You might want to put some tape on the nose of the ball to protect it.)

## Footwork

Footwork is also integrated into the release. **Footwork comes down to the most basic thing—stepping toward your target as you pass. Stepping toward your target will help you not only with power but also with accuracy as well. The better your footwork, the stronger you will be in passing the ball. If you have a good strong setup, step to your target, push off that back foot, bring that shoulder through, rotate those hips, and throw with your foot going toward the target then you will be more powerful and more accurate.** You'll actually amass more power because you're getting your whole body

**A pass is more than just an arm motion; it incorporates the whole body, beginning with the legs. Incorporate properly timed leg, body, and arm motions into your passing method and you'll greatly increase your power and accuracy.**

involved. If you do it with proper timing and discipline, you'll play a lot stronger than you really are. We don't pass the ball just using the arm. We really pass the ball with our whole body. It starts with your feet and goes all the way up to your fingers. In the DVD, coach **Bruce Arians** (Peyton Manning's longtime quarterback coach) says there are three skill sets needed for good passing; the short powerful motions of a boxer, the hip action of a golfer, and the high, circular motion made by the arm of a tennis player on his serve.

Basically the ball is coming out of your hand as you're in your motion of stepping. Then from there your arm and body follow through in a relaxed mode. The more relaxed your body is

during and immediately after a pass, the better it can absorb a hit from a defender.

**TIPS**

■ Upper arm parallel
  to the ground
■ Step toward the target
■ Palm turns outward
■ Thumb swings around from
  pointing inward to outward

## Passing on the Run

We already talked about the importance of foot-work and turning your shoulders toward the target. But when you and/or your receiver are on the move, how do you know where to put the ball? There are a couple of basic rules of thumb you'll want to keep in mind.

When you're on the move and your receiver is on the move and you're running in the same direction, place the ball slightly in front of him, no further out than arm's reach.

When you're on the move and he is stationary, throw it about a yard inside your target and the ball will move toward the target due to the momentum of the passer.

If the receiver is moving downfield away from you towards the sideline and you're moving towards the sideline, the ball will have a tendency to float in the direction you are running, so

account for that. Assuming your receiver is open, you need to guard against throwing the ball out of bounds. Try to keep the ball in bounds because the ball is going to drift on you. Use the boundary as a guideline to keep the ball in. Just think of keeping the ball in play and still putting it downfield for him. At least then you're going to give him a chance to catch the ball. How many long passes have you seen where quarterbacks on the move throw the ball out of bounds? It's because they don't use that theory.

When you are on the move in one direction and the receiver is moving back inside in the opposite direction, lead him much more than normal—about double the usual lead. This pass is risky because it puts both the quarterback and the receiver in the position of being blindsided by a defender.

Passing on the run can be a great weapon for a young guy, because let's face it, in junior high and high school breakdowns in pass protection and/or missed assignments often force you to throw such passes. On a more positive note, passing on the run is a real good way to take advantage of your athletic and mental skills. If you can run well and pass well and you can make good decisions on the move then you will be invaluable to your team.

There are a handful of key fundamentals concerning passing on the run. One is, as we talked earlier, the footwork coming out from under the center—pushing off and accelerating full speed to a certain point, then coasting and then passing.

Another key to throwing on the run is being under control. If you run full speed and try to pass the ball at full speed, you're not going to be anywhere near as accurate as if you were under control. Now somebody might say, "Well, what if someone is chasing you?" Well, that's just a common sense thing. Of course, you're going to move a little faster if you know somebody is riding on your tail, but most of the time when you're passing on the run you *don't know* who's chasing you.

Some coaches tell their quarterbacks not to throw on the run but to pull up, stop running, and then throw. I don't agree with that. The reason why you're moving is to get away from pressure—to get into the open where you know you're spreading the field and you're able to see. I've always believed in passing on the run, but I teach my quarterbacks to run and throw at a speed that keeps them under control. The danger in pulling up and stopping is that there may be a freight train chasing you.

**The key to accuracy when passing on the run is turning your shoulders towards the target. A lot of quarterbacks confuse that with pointing their feet toward the target. While it's easy and right to step toward your target when throwing a dropback pass, it's not necessary on the run. In fact, if you're rolling out and you want to throw the ball, if you try to step toward your target you'll probably fall over.**

I was pretty good at throwing on the run. I

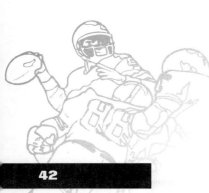

could be moving along and be outside the pocket and throw the ball back inside at a pretty good angle and complete the pass because of my shoulders. My feet were balanced but they were moving parallel to the line of scrimmage, and I turned my shoulders toward my target. Your feet have to be balanced underneath you. But those shoulders turning and the timing of your upper body releasing the pass gives you the strength.

Now, I've said I like for my quarterbacks to pass on the run, but it's important to point out that there are a few things NOT to do. For instance, I see a lot of young quarterbacks running to their right and then trying to throw all the way back across the field to the left. That is not smart football. The problem is that with all your energy driving you to the right it takes enormous strength to make the ball fly accurately to the left. Very often this kind of bad pass attempt is forced because of pressure. In many cases these passes will result in an interception. If you're rolling out and you're under heavy pressure, 99 percent of the time you're better off throwing the ball away. If it's against the rules to throw it outside the pocket, then throw it at a receiver's feet or run and save whatever yardage you can.

As for throwing the ball, say, into the middle of the field—that can be a very accurate and productive throw. What often happens is that you have defenders moving along the line of scrimmage with you and they overrun

receivers, leaving the offense with relatively easy yardage.

**For a passer who's right-handed, running to your left can be just as accurate as running the other way, as long as you emphasize turning your shoulders. When you're in the pocket and you're protected, you can use your feet and shoulders to determine where you're going to pass the ball. When you're on the run you can really only rely on your shoulders. The feet are busy moving you and balancing you. When you make the throw, you turn your hips and your shoulders toward your target. You turn your whole torso except your feet, and your feet keep moving.**

## TIPS

- Throw under control
- Keep moving
- Turn shoulders toward target

## *Types of Passes*

Not all passes are created equal. There are many different types of passes used in many different situations.

### *Swing Pass*

One of the more difficult types of passes to throw is one that most casual fans take for granted: the swing pass. This is a short pass

that flies roughly parallel to the line of scrimmage. Given how short this pass is, it has a very high incompletion rate. That's because most quarterbacks don't work on it enough and therefore don't know where to throw it. With a downfield pass a quarterback can always lead the receiver—that is, throw to where the receiver will be. That works because on a downfield pass the receiver and the defenders are all running in the same direction. On a swing pass the intended receiver is running toward the sideline, a little downfield, and the defenders are rushing upfield right at him. If the quarterback puts too much lead on the ball, the receiver will get demolished. The trick is not to over-lead the receiver. I've always told my quarterbacks that on a swing pass they are to pass the ball to the receiver's downfield shoulder. Don't over-lead the guy, and of course, don't throw it behind him.

## Over-the-Middle Pass

Another type of pass is the short over-the-middle pass. This is another pass where, unlike the downfield pass, you're not leading the receiver very much. When throwing over the middle you want to keep the ball flight about chest-high. That way you're protecting the receiver from oncoming defenders. Usually when a guy is running across the middle he's under control because he's going through a lot of traffic. So don't over-lead him. In order to make sure that he doesn't have to really stretch out, just throw

a dart straight in there, the same principle as the little swing pass.

### Sideline Pass

The sideline pass is where you really need to have good footwork, because it's usually a longer and riskier throw. Unlike the other touch passes described above, the sideline pass is all about strength. You want to zoom the ball in there. If you lob a sideline pass, you'll not only throw an interception, but it's likely to be returned for a touchdown.

On sideline passes I've always told my quarterbacks to plan for a completion but account for an incompletion. That is, throw a pass that your receiver has a chance of catching but favor the outside (the sideline side) of his body. That way, if you miss your target you'll miss him to the outside and the ball will land harmlessly out of bounds. A miss to the inside would increase the chances of a very dangerous interception.

When throwing sideline passes, you need to put some zip on the ball. In such instances I tell my quarterbacks to "aim at the receiver's helmet." Now why throw at the helmet? Won't it go over the receiver's head? No. All passes travel on an arc, meaning about halfway to the target the ball begins to drop. So if I'm throwing the ball 25 yards to the sideline (the receiver is 12-15 yards downfield and I'm 10 yards behind the line of scrimmage), about 12 yards after I release the ball it is going to start dropping. So if I aim at helmet level, then I've got a good chance for the ball to settle in there about chest-high. Trust me, receivers will love you for this. If the ball is at their feet they have very little chance of making the catch, but if you put the ball chin-high it'll be a lot easier to pull it in.

## Comeback Pass

Any pass where the receiver is moving back toward the quarterback—a hook pass, a curl pass—is a comeback pass. Coaches have taught different techniques on these for years. Some coaches say put the ball to the receiver's right, others say put it to his left or put it low. I missed a receiver on a comeback once, and I had all kinds of excuses about where I was try-ing to put the ball. My coach said—and I'll never forgot it—"Just hit him in the numbers." You know what? He was right. If there's some-body in the way and you can't see the numbers, you shouldn't be passing it anyway.

## The Corner Route

The most difficult pass is the corner route, where the receiver goes downfield and then breaks out toward "the corner." Here you really need to depend on your coach and the way he teaches the route. The most difficult thing about throwing a corner route is knowing pre-cisely what corner we're talking about and when the receiver is supposed to break toward it. Is the break 25 yards downfield? Is it 30 yards? Is the receiver heading for the back cor-ner, the front corner, the left, or the right? Is it an imaginary corner? Things get even more

complicated when a defender enters the picture as you may have to round off the pattern. So the coach has to help the quarterback and the receiver in defining the parameters of the route.

Once you've worked with your coach to define the route, the trick to throwing a good corner route is picking up the angle of the receiver. You may have to wait a fraction of a second longer than you want to before you throw the ball, but if you try to anticipate the receiver and you throw it as he's making his break, you had better be on the same page. If he makes his break any sooner or later than you're expecting you could be in big trouble.

When I was coaching in the NFL I used to attend the NFL Combine (a camp held every winter in Indianapolis where NFL hopefuls go to show coaches and scouts their skills). I used to sit up in the stands and watch these young quarterbacks. There would be no defenders, just quarterbacks and receivers. Each quarterback would throw to two or three receivers and then the next quarterback would step in. Overall, they'd be hitting their receivers about nine out of ten times. They'd be completing sideline passes, over-the-middle passes, and roll-outs. When it came time for the corner routes, I would take bets that even without defenders these quarterbacks were not going to complete fifty percent of these routes. And they wouldn't. Why? Because the corner route takes the team-work of the coach, the quarterback, and the receiver. Use a quarterback and receiver who've

never played together and it just won't work.
The receiver will run the route one way, and the
quarterback will plan for it a different way.

## The Post Route

To me, the post route is like the corner route.
You, the quarterback, better know the angle on
which the receiver is planning to break. What
I've always tried to do on a post route is have
the receiver and the passer on the same page by
always using the same landmark—the middle
of the goal post. Now, no matter where you're
running and no matter where you see the
receiver running, you know that's where he's
going to end up. Then the quarterback only has
to make one decision: Whether or not to throw
the ball, depending on the coverage. This puts
the quarterback and the receiver on the same
page and raises their level of confidence.

## The Bomb

One of the best long-ball passers in recent NFL
history is Chris Chandler. The surprising thing
is that five years into his pro career he was one
of the worst long-ball passers in the league.
When he came to the Arizona Cardinals he had
a strong arm. He'd put it out there 50, 60, 70
yards with very pretty ball flight. The only
trouble was that he rarely completed any of
these long balls, even in practice. After one
particular season he made up his mind that
he wanted to learn more about throwing the
long ball.

Chris is a very smart guy, without a doubt

one of the smartest quarterbacks I've ever coached. In 1992, he said, "Teach me." I said, "Okay, the very first thing you're going to learn is how to throw the long ball." He said, "I can throw the long ball." And I said, "Yeah, you can throw it a long way—incomplete." I told him that there's a trick to throwing the long ball successfully—"Hit the guy."

It's not how far you throw the ball, it's whether you hit the guy or not. Whether he's 20, 30, or 40 yards down the field it's all about completing the pass. The quarterback has to do a good job of making the ball catchable. It's not about throwing over the receiver's left shoulder or right shoulder. Just put it out in front of him enough where he can catch the ball on the run. I know it sounds simple, but we began to work on that and he became one of the best long-ball passers in the league. It's just because he learned that it wasn't how far you throw it or whether you throw it over the receiver's outside shoulder or inside shoulder. You go back, you read the defense and then you put the ball on the proper arc (depending on how far you need to throw it) so he can go catch it on the move. I didn't make technique changes, I just changed the way Chris perceived what he had to do— the mentality. Why was **Joe Montana**—who did not have a real strong arm—such a good long-ball passer? Because he had the right mentality: Complete the pass. Let's not show off and see how far we can throw it or how high we can throw it. Instead, let's see how accurate we can be. Let's see how catchable the pass can be.

Years later, in 1995, Chris came within one pass of throwing the most perfect game in the history of the NFL (as measured by quarter-back rating). He completed 23 of 25 passes for 450 yards, 4 touchdowns, and no interceptions in a game against the Cincinnati Bengals. He must have completed 5 or 6 bombs that day, doing exactly what we had worked on back in Phoenix 4 years earlier.

# *Drills*

### ✓*1. Stationary Targets*

Coaches Tip

**Track 13**

I believe in stationary targets. You do not need to have moving targets all the time. You can take receivers and put them on the sideline right where the ball should be thrown. Just have them put their hands out and stand there. You can do it with a coach, a fellow player, a buddy, even your mother. When I was in high school, my girlfriend would go out to the practice field with me when I couldn't get anybody else. She would put on gloves and hold up a trash can lid, and I would throw the ball at the lid. That way, she didn't have to catch the ball, and we didn't have to worry about chasing it. In the old days, a lot of guys would hang an old tire from a tree. The only problem with that is that you

have to chase the ball. Ideally you want to create a situation where you don't have to spend valuable practice time chasing down the ball.

## ✓ 2. Moving Targets

When I was a kid, my friend and I—he played quarterback, too—would go out to this park that had a little road that went all the way around it. One of us would get on one side of the road and the other would get on the other side of the road. And we would trot all the way around the park playing catch on the run—turning our shoulders, throwing the ball, catching it, throwing it, just staying on the move. About halfway around, we'd stop and start in the other direction. So we were able to get our conditioning in at the same time we practiced throwing on the run.

Another thing we used to do was play imaginary games. We took turns being the receiver and the passer. Every time we would go the length of the field and score a touchdown, it was a touchdown for "our team." Whenever we had an incomplete pass, the "other team" would be credited with a touchdown. Whichever side reached 72 points first was the winner. That means we went up and down the field a minimum of twelve times. That's 1,200 yards worth of passes to each other! We'd throw every kind of pass imaginable, and we played this game right into college. In fact, during my senior season at Tulsa, two of my receivers were **Howard Twilley** and Eddie Fletcher. Prior to the 1964 season, we spent four days playing this game. At one point, we went *two straight days* without

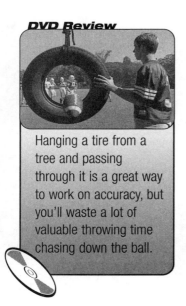

**DVD Review**

Hanging a tire from a tree and passing through it is a great way to work on accuracy, but you'll waste a lot of valuable throwing time chasing down the ball.

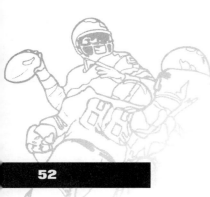

the ball hitting the ground. That year, Howard set the record for most receptions in a season by a college receiver. That record still stands.

### ✓ 3. Throwing on the Run

One drill that I did with quarterbacks—I used it with Mark Rypien a lot—was we'd stand anywhere from 10 to 30 yards apart. Mark would circle around me throwing on the run, and I would catch it and throw it back to him. And he'd just keep circling, pass and go back the other way. That was a nice way to reinforce the feel of throwing on the run.

### ✓ 4. The Scramble

For quarterbacks in pro ball I used the scramble drill. I'd have the quarterback drop back, scramble out of the pocket, and then one receiver would be on one side of the field and another on the other side. Each time the quarterback would scramble, the receiver would do something different. The receiver would run deep, stop and go inside, or run to the sideline. But each time he would do something different. This drill accomplishes two things. First, it forces the quarterback to learn to adjust under pressure, but it also makes him focus on the body language of each receiver. The better the quarterback can pick up a receiver's intentions the more successful he'll be.

**Whatever drills you come up with on your own, try to make them fun. Remember, football is a game. It shouldn't be drudgery.**

# ChapterFour

# Footwork

## The Proper Dropback

From 1983-87 I was the quarterback coach for the Washington Redskins. During that time a kid named Mark Rypien was coming out of college. At 6-feet, 4-inches and 230 pounds, he was a big, strong guy. But the word around the league was that he was just too slow. He simply didn't have very quick feet.

I went up to Washington State, where Mark had played his college ball, and I watched all his game films. Then I worked him out. I was extremely impressed with his intelligence, his arm strength, and his footwork technique. He just didn't have the quick feet you look for in a quarterback. So, we drafted him, but in one of the later rounds. I had a couple years with him where he was just a third-string guy. I spent a lot of time during practice working with him alone. We spent a lot of time on his footwork and delivery. But mostly we focused on his foot speed, jumping rope and doing quickness drills.

By 1991, Mark had become one of the quickest dropback quarterbacks in NFL history, and he earned Super Bowl MVP honors that season. He was very strong in the pocket—nothing bothered him. In '89, '90, and '91— those 3 or 4 years when he was playing with the Washington Redskins—the hard work paid off. Mark went from being the tortoise to the hare. The thing was that all through high school and college, Mark was bigger and stronger than the other kids, and since he was successful, no one paid

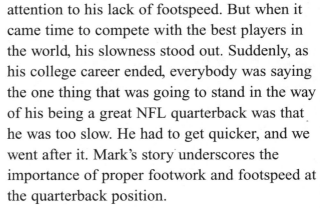

attention to his lack of footspeed. But when it came time to compete with the best players in the world, his slowness stood out. Suddenly, as his college career ended, everybody was saying the one thing that was going to stand in the way of his being a great NFL quarterback was that he was too slow. He had to get quicker, and we went after it. Mark's story underscores the importance of proper footwork and footspeed at the quarterback position.

**NOTE:** Always follow your coach's teaching on footwork, and use these tips as a supplement. The golden rule of footwork is "Take Short, Quick Steps." Long strides work great for open field running, but in a crowded backfield when you're trying to hand-off safely or scramble to avoid a sack, long strides get you in trouble. You get spread out too much. **Short, quick, precise steps are the answer**. With those short steps, the emphasis should be on quickness and not on length. You should always be in a balanced position with that ball tucked away.

The more you're like a matador the better. Watch how a bullfighter moves his feet and steps aside as the bull comes by. The bull just brushes against the matador. There's room to clear, but it all starts with good footwork.

By the way, I don't think there's a better way to increase the quickness of your feet than jumping rope. I believe jumping rope is one of the best things that you can possibly do, because like in football, if you don't move your

**Jumping rope may be the best way to improve quickness. It did wonders for Mark Rypien, who went from being a slow QB to a fleet-footed Super Bowl MVP.**

feet, you're going to end up on the ground. Jumping rope played a huge role in Mark Rypien's turnaround. Mark jumped rope all the time. After we got off the practice field, he'd go into the weight room and pick up that jump rope and go to work.

Another great way to improve footwork is high-stepping. In college and in the NFL they have rope beds where the players high-step in and out of the square holes made by the rope. Of course, not many kids are going to have one of these in their backyards, but you can create

your own by finding eight or ten spare tires and lining them up side by side and high-stepping through them. Go through backwards and forwards—use your imagination. One of the great things about football is that you don't have to go to a store and you don't have to spend a lot of money to train. You can go find some old tires, or rig up your own rope bed. Using chalk, you might even draw a grid on your driveway and hopscotch through it.

## Passing Footwork

### The 3-Step Drop

You're under center. The play calls for you to take the snap, move away from center, and throw the ball. Rule No. 1: Don't crowd the center with your feet. In other words, have your feet positioned a good distance from the center. I tell my players to put their feet as far from the line of scrimmage as possible while remaining balanced and under control. Why? Centers and other offensive linemen are notorious for stepping slightly backwards upon the snap of the ball. A quarterback who's careless about his foot position at the snap is bound to get his feet stomped on periodically. So make sure your feet are as far away as you can get them while still remaining balanced and under control. I also suggest that you keep your feet equally distanced from the center rather than in a staggered position with one foot up and one foot back.

As I mentioned earlier, **stand as tall as you can**, don't be all hunched over. Now you're in a good starting position to get away from the center. You'll be able to see better and move more quickly.

**The Drop Back**

**Track 15**

**If you're right-handed (simply reverse for lefties) once you get the ball, push off your left foot. DO NOT lift the left foot, simply push off of it. Your first real step is your right foot coming away from the line of scrimmage. It's basically a short step back, with your toes of your right foot pointing toward the sideline. Then the left foot crosses over. Then the right crosses behind. You plant the right foot, step toward your target and throw. 1, 2, 3, throw!**

Some coaches teach a system of one long step and two short steps or two short steps and one long step. I've always felt that that's just too mechanical. With pass footwork you want a quick, common sense getaway: Three steps, stand up, step toward your target and throw the ball. Watch the DVD to see how Drew Bledsoe executes the 3-, 5- and 7-step drops.

Note that above, after the three steps the next instruction is STAND up, not step up. Stepping up is something you do on a dropback pass when you're stepping up in the pocket. But on a short , 3-step drop, *standing up* is more important than stepping up. When you stand up you can see more of the field. You can also deliver the ball in whatever direction you choose because you've got good posture, you're balanced, and you can take your step and move toward the target. If you don't stand up, you lose 3 or 4 more inches of visibility. It hurts your downfield vision and diminishes your balance.

For example, suppose you're playing catch and you're throwing the ball back and forth. You're accurate, you're hitting the guy, and you've got nice zip on the ball. Look at your posture. The odds are you're pretty much standing up. That's the way to deliver a football. Stand up and be tall.

**TIPS**
- Take short steps
- Protect the ball
- Stand tall
- 1-2-3, step, throw

### The 5-Step Drop

The 5-step drop works the same way—it's just that you're taking two more steps. Now the fifth step can be taught two ways. One is you just hit your last step and stand and deliver the football. **The other option is for young quarterbacks who typically don't have enough strength to throw the ball without fully regaining their balance and posture. They may need to take a short little shuffle step upfield. By shuffling up a step some of their weight gets back on**

their front foot making it easier to throw. In other words the right foot hits, the weight is back on the right foot and then as he stands tall he puts the weight back on the left foot and he brings that right foot back up and he's totally staying balanced.

## The 7-Step Drop

The 7-step drop is utilized on long pass plays. It give the receivers time to get down the field and also allows the offensive line time to build a pocket. The footwork is fundamentally the same as the 5-step drop, you're just taking two additional steps **and shuffling up toward the line of scrimmage**. You're shuffling up for two reasons: One is you're regaining your balance. Since you've gone seven steps, you're moving away from the play at a pretty good clip. The second reason for the shuffle up is that by the time you hit that last step defenders are likely to be rushing in on you. But once you move up into the pocket you've changed the target and enhanced your protection. The defenders' momentum is now working against them. They're going up the field, and you're moving toward the line of scrimmage.

One of the worst mistakes a quarterback can make is to try to run out the back end of the pocket. Do that and suddenly the defensive player's momentum is working in his own favor and you've lost your pass protection. You're eventually going to get dragged down for a 12-yard loss, and the linemen are going to say,

**DVD Review**

The Drop Back is basically a short step back, with your toes of your right foot pointing toward the sideline. Then the left foot crosses over. Then the right crosses behind. You plant the right foot, step toward your target, and throw. 1, 2, 3, throw!

"I didn't know he was going to be that deep." Step up into the pocket and get into that little niche of protection. It's not easy. One of the most difficult things for a quarterback is to feel comfortable in that pocket area—the eye of the hurricane—and discern what's going on down-field. That's hard to teach, but that's the secret to being a pocket passer.

Troy Aikman was a tremendous pocket passer. Mark Rypien was also great in the pocket. Size certainly doesn't hurt in this area. Ironically, **Dan Fouts** had awful footwork; instead of crossing over he was a real backped-dler, but he did have a knack for standing right in the pocket. Once he got into that little niche he was really good. **Roman Gabriel** was also really good at that. Today, I would say both Peyton Manning and Drew Bledsoe are both very strong in the pocket.

One thing I see in a lot of young quarter-backs today is that when they set up in the pocket they bounce all over the place, hopping up and down on their toes like a kid beside an ice cream truck. I have never coached a quar-terback to do that. First, I think a quarterback needs to feel natural back there and do whatev-er feels most comfortable. I just let him go back and if he shuffles his feet a little bit, so be it. As coach Carl Smith explains in the DVD, if you do move your feet, "don't let your cleats come out of the grass." Keep them close to the surface. That way as soon as the opportunity to throw the ball arises, you can fire without hav-

ing to reset your feet. If a coach *makes* a guy either do that or not do that, pretty soon all he's worrying about is whether he's making his feet go up and down. It becomes just another thing to think about.

## Steps on the Run

Whether it's a rollout pass or an option, the basic footwork used in moving away from the center is much the same. You need to push off of one foot and place the other in the direction you're headed. That push-off foot should be just that, a push off. Don't pick it up first, just push off. Everything is quicker from the line of scrimmage by just having a push-off.

After that it's a full-speed sprint to a spot predetermined by the play. Once you reach that spot—which is usually just outside the tight end—you go into a coast. Remember, no one does a good job of throwing on the move at full speed, so it's full speed at first to get outside the pocket, then when you've created separation between yourself and the defense, level off and coast under control.

And like what we learned earlier: When you're running, the ball should be close to your body for protection. I hold it with two hands chest-high, and as I step the ball moves back and forth from the right side of my chest to the left side of my chest.

# ChapterFive

# Mental Toughness

## Using Your Head

**G**enerally speaking, who does best in school: kids who study or kids who don't study? Now who is most likely to play a sport well, kids who study the game or kids who don't? There's a lot more to being good at a sport than simply playing it. Sure, as a kid in a pickup game, it's enough to make a great throw or a great catch, but the guys who excel in high school, college, and eventually the pros are the ones who treat the game like a subject, not only playing but also reading and learning as much as they can off the field.

How can you become a student of the game? Read books about football and football players. As you get a little older, you'll probably have the opportunity to watch films of your own team and your opposition. Listen to your coaches as they go through those films. Ask questions and take notes. Reading this book makes you a student of the game. The more you know, the better chance you've got to be a successful player.

Quarterbacks are asked a lot of questions by a lot of different people. Your teammates are going to ask you, "What are we doing on this play?" or "What do I do on this play?" and you have to be the teacher. The coach is on the sidelines, he's done his job. **On the field, you have to be the authority.** I can remember in high school and college ball I had all kinds of signals I'd use behind my back to help out my running backs. If they forgot the play or the snap count or the direction they were supposed to run, I'd put my hand

back there and point this way or that way.

Do you like to watch football on television? That's great, but instead of absent-mindedly gazing at the tube, a student of the game will pay close attention to what the announcers say about each coach's strategy. If a team runs a certain play, try to figure out why they made that decision. Obviously the most important source of information is your coach, but you can augment what you learn from him with what you see and hear in other games.

As a coach I've always tried to tell my players not only WHAT to do but WHY we were doing it. What is the strategy behind this formation or play? Why are we making this adjustment? If a player asks "Why?" I think that's a sign of interest, a sign that he cares. I think a lot of times coaches just assume that kids know the answer. If a coach says, "I want you to take the ball and sprint right, towards the defensive end. Then I want you to fake the pitch and cut inside," sometimes you might need to know why to do that. Fact is you'll probably do it better if you know why you're doing it. (The entire burden here is not on the coach. The player has to take on the responsibility of asking good questions in a polite manner and at the right time.) Asking good questions will put all the pieces together for you. Then you will know what the coaches are thinking during the play on the sideline, what they're looking for, and why they called a particular play at a particular time.

One of the most successful quarterbacks in the game today may be the most ardent student of the game that I have ever been around. **Kurt Warner** of the St. Louis Rams is really sharp, and he appreciates the game. That's probably due to the road he had to travel to get where he is today. He was a castoff and ended up being an Arena League quarterback. Then he went over to Europe to play, and it looked like the NFL didn't believe in him. He had a million-to-one shot of getting into the NFL. He clawed his way to stardom by studying, practicing, and learning all he could about playing football.

That analytical, academic appreciation for the game can take you a long way. I would not have had a college or NFL career without that analytical ability. That's what gave me the edge. I got along very well with Cowboys head coach **Tom Landry** because I had the same kind of analytical mind. Dallas quarterbacks **Craig Morton** and **Don Meredith** didn't think in this way. They preferred to just go play football. The only way I was ever able to compete with them was by using the analytical approach and studying the game. That was the coach in me. My father was a coach, and so I grew up understanding that I needed every edge that I could get.

## Can You Adjust?

Can you adjust? Are you a quick thinker? You better be if you want to play quarterback.

Between the snap of the ball and the time you have to throw it, the average quarterback has no more than 3.5 seconds. So there's a lot of decision-making done in that short period of time. Now you can see where the "student of the game" aspect I mentioned earlier pays off. It's all in preparation for making quick, correct decisions. Very often in football and other sports, the difference between winning and losing is making quick, correct decisions and adjustments.

Here's an example: A pass rush is coming in, and the play calls for you to roll right. But you've got a guy who's six feet tall coming at you from the right. How do you adjust?

That's one type of adjustment, trying to turn a loss into a gain. Green Bay Packers quarterback **Brett Favre** is great at that. He's probably one of the quickest thinkers and quickest adjusters in the game.

Adjustments can also be made by coaches on the sideline. For instance the coaches may have entered a game thinking their opponent was going to play a certain defense. But as the game unfolds the opponent springs a different defense on them. In that case, the coaches will have to make an adjustment to account for this unexpected defense. When I was in high school we played a game in which the opposing defense was "stacking the line"—placing more players on the defensive line of scrimmage than we expected them to. We immediately had to start making adjustments. The coach (also my father) was on top of the situation. He had a board on the sideline, and he got the guys together and starting drawing up special formations to take advantage of what they were doing. We made an adjustment using two new plays and wiped them out because they couldn't adjust to our adjustment.

You can adjust technique, you can adjust play calling, and you can adjust alignment. There are all kinds of places for a quarterback to make adjustments—with the approval of his coach, of course. Most casual observers see football as a rigid series of planned plays, but there is a real creativity in the game, and it shows in critical adjustments.

## TIPS

- ■ Be a student of the game
- ■ Ask why
- ■ Learn to adjust

## Handling The Pressure

Quarterback is without a doubt the most visible position on a football team. That can be fun, but it also means pressure. When a team is struggling the first two targets of criticism are usually the head coach and the quarterback—not necessarily in that order. Pressure comes in two forms: physical and mental.

### *Physical Pressure*

Physical pressure is fairly obvious. It's the feeling you get when time after time, pass protection breaks down and you're forced to run for your life from guys who outweigh you by 80 to 100 pounds. They're coming from everywhere. You've got to be able to handle that feeling because many times the demons in your brain are telling you, "Oh you can't handle this, there are too many of them, they're coming from everywhere."

Well, they're not really coming from everywhere. One guy is beating his man so we have to block that one guy, or they're coming from the right side because they're overloading. We have to take one more blocker to the right. That's handling the physical pressure by staying cool and making a reasoned adjustment.

Now, if you're under pressure and you've got three seconds or so to decide where you're going to throw the ball, it certainly helps if you've been dedicated and analytical enough to know where all your receivers are going to be at a given instant. If you don't know that and you're three seconds into the play, forget it.

When I played football I was an overachiever, but physically I shouldn't have been able to do the things I did. My ability to adjust and my understanding of the game were the foundations of my career as a quarterback and laid the foundation for my career as a quarterback coach and offensive coordinator.

**Physical pressure is the feeling you get when pass protection breaks down and you're forced to run for your life.**

## Mental Pressure

There's a certain pressure that comes with a 6-foot 5-inch 290-pounder coming at you. But there's another more insidious pressure that most quarterbacks eventually have to deal with: mental pressure. Being under physical pressure to avoid a tackle or make a play is one thing. Mental pressure, those conversations we have in our heads when we question our ability ("Can I do this?") or experience stage-fright ("Oh my goodness, everybody is watching") or deal with other people's expectations ("Everybody is expecting me to do this"). Remember, no one is expecting you to do it by yourself. You have a team and coaches, all of whom are working together to make the play happen. A quarterback can feel alone sometimes, but he never is. Just step into that huddle and say, "We are going to do this."

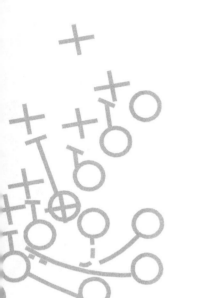

The ability to step into a huddle and put aside your nerves (or at least hide them) and make your teammates feel confident in your ability and in their ability to perform is called poise. A poised quarterback steps into the huddle during a pressure situation and says in a calm voice, "Guys, all we have to do is make this first down and we win. We're going to run this play over you, Charlie. You're going to blow a hole wide open for Tommy." That quick, calm pep talk can make the difference between winning and losing.

One element of poise is never getting too excited during good times and never getting too tight during rough times. That way when the "kitchen" gets really hot—meaning the game or the season is on the line—you can step up and make the right decisions. A quarterback who is too emotionally charged by a game's events may have a hard time clearing his head when decision and execution time comes. STAY COOL!

Look at some of the great names ever to play quarterback. Troy Aikman was extremely poised. Nothing got him excited. Doug Williams was a very cool and calm person. Today, Kurt Warner is extremely cool and poised. The great ones have a gift. In situations where most people would be getting tense, breathing faster, raising their blood pressure, guys like Kurt go the opposite way. They seem to breathe slower, think more clearly, and execute more precisely. It's been that way through-

out the history of the game. Look back at **Otto Graham**, he was the same way. It seemed like Graham was always making the plays when the pressure was on and he *had to* make the plays. It was the same with **Johnny Unitas**; that was his whole thing, making the play when it had to be made. And **Bobby Layne** was one of the first great modern-day quarterbacks. He didn't have great stats, but he threw touchdown passes at the right time. For all these guys, the heavier the pressure, the better they played.

## Concentration

Concentration means staying focused on the game and paying attention to the details. Some guys will start looking at the crowd. A few guys might watch the cheerleaders. But the guys who are going places stay focused on the game. That focus might take the form of a few quiet moments and a cold drink in between series. It might mean a conversation with your position coach. It might simply mean rooting for the defense. The key is that you're keeping your mind in the game, staying loose and staying focused.

In youth football and even in high school, kids are likely to be talking about anything from the movie they went to yesterday to their mother's new car. As a quarterback, a team leader, you can't fall into that trap, and if your teammates do, you need to snap them out of it. Few things tell a coach more clearly that a play-

er is not interested in football than when he sees a kid on the sideline talking about something that has nothing to do with football. I've seen situations where it's third down and nine yards to go, we're getting ready to punt and a guy who's on the punt coverage team is chatting about his post-game plans. **In my years of coaching I've often found that the guys who daydream on the field or on the bench are the same guys who daydream at home or in school. They're not finishers.**

I hate to admit it but it happened to me once. I was a rookie and we were playing the New York Giants in Yankee Stadium. It was about 15 degrees and the wind was blowing; it was one of those awful days in New York. Like a lot of backup quarterbacks, I was designated the holder for field goals and extra points. Back then we had poor heaters on the benches, so we had big sideline capes to keep us warm. Naturally, I kept my cape buttoned up all nice and warm. Well, our offense got down to the Giants' 5-yard line. So, figuring we were either going to score a touchdown or kick a field goal, I got ready. Off went the cape, in I went and we kicked our extra point. I came back and got my nice warm cape on. Well, on the ensuing kickoff, the Giants fumbled the ball, and we ran it in for a touchdown. So I had to go in for another extra point, but this time I couldn't get the cape off. The snap at the top, near my neck, wouldn't come undone. I yanked my helmet off and tried to pull it over the top of my head. At one point, I was on the ground pulling on this thing. I looked up and there was Coach Landry standing there watching me. He said, "Are you about ready?" I was choking to death, and everybody was laughing. So the equipment manager came over and finally got it loose. I ran out on the field and everybody was asking, "Where were you?" I told them I was choking to death on the sidelines in front of Landry.

That's a humorous example of what lack of planning and lack of focus can mean during a game. Now, if you stay too intensely focused for the whole game, you'll burn out. *It is a game*. This is not a court of law we're talking about here. Football is fun and you should have fun playing it. So how do you mix focus with fun? That's easy. The game itself is fun enough for real players. Being on the field, working with your teammates and your coaches to win the game, that's fun. Sure, you can a have a few laughs with your teammates during practice and games, but never let silliness, horseplay or carelessness enter the picture. Concentration is nothing more than caring about what you're trying to do, caring enough so that distractions just aren't as compelling.

I've noticed that the guys who concentrate best are the guys who do it all the time—not only on the field, but at home and in their schoolwork. You need to make concentration a way of life if you're ever really going to benefit from it. There are a lot of quarterbacks who expect that they can slough off all day in school

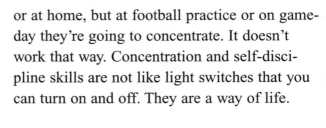

or at home, but at football practice or on game-day they're going to concentrate. It doesn't work that way. Concentration and self-discipline skills are not like light switches that you can turn on and off. They are a way of life.

## *Punctuality*

In a literal sense punctuality means being on time, but it really means more than that. It means respect. If a coach tells you he wants to see you at 3:00 and you show up at 3:06, he's got a right to think that you don't consider him and what he has to say very important. Punctuality also means preparation. If you're on time it means you made the necessary preparations. In my mind, being punctual actually means being a little early. If you wait until the last minute to show up for something important a lot of things can go wrong to make you late and make a bad impression. In my book, 3:00 means 2:45. You may have to sit around for 15 minutes, but getting there early will not only save you a lot of stress, it'll tell coaches, teachers, bosses—whoever is expecting you—that you respect them and that you care about the meeting or the appointment.

I learned that lesson the hard way back in 1965 when I was a rookie with the Cowboys. I missed a quarterback meeting that year. One day Craig Morton, Don Meredith, myself, and another rookie showed up for our 11:00 am team meeting. After the meeting Coach Landry

called us all over and said, "I'm going to fine each of you $200." I said, "For what?" He said, "You didn't come to the quarterback meeting this morning." Meredith said, "What quarterback meeting? You never told us anything about a quarterback meeting." Landry said, "We have one every year on the Monday we come back from training camp." Meredith looked at him and said, "You're fining us for not remembering that we had a meeting last year at 9:00 am on the Monday when we came back from training camp?" And Landry said, "Yes."

That might have been unfair, but it taught me a lesson. For the rest of my career I always checked to see when meetings were scheduled, and I never missed another one.

## TIPS

- Identify the source of pressure
- Don't expect to do it yourself
- Don't get too high or too low
- Stay focused on the game
- Be early

# ChapterSix

# Eyes, Ears, and Voice

## Use Your Senses

I think the eyes may be the most important physical asset for a quarterback. You can be the strongest passer in history, but if you don't have good eyes, you're never going to be a good player. It's your vision and the decisions you make based on that vision that make the difference between winning and losing. Now, not all kids are born with great eyes or great vision. That's okay, because young quarterbacks need to be trained by their coaches. We all use our eyes everyday, but a quarterback needs to be trained to use his eyes specifically as a quarterback. For instance, the primary tendency for young athletes playing almost any sport is to look down. Most great players acquire the ability to keep their eyes up. That sort of thing takes training.

It's important that all football players, from the time they break the huddle, have a firm plan in mind on every play. As a quarterback (and for most other positions) that plan starts with your eyes.

Coaches Tip

Track 21

What are you going to look for? What will your eyes tell the defense about your intentions? When you go back to throw a pass, what are you looking at? Are you just going back and looking around, "window-shopping," or are you looking for the right things? Are you remembering those things so that you can use that information in the next series?

The eyes may very well be a ▶ quarterback's most valuable tool. Make sure that from the time you step out of the huddle until the time the play is blown dead you're taking in everything the defense is giving you.

Don't just gaze into space while standing over center, try to decipher the defense's intentions, take note of where defenders, particularly the secondary is positioned. This information can be enormously helpful in reading defenses.

I have had professional quarterbacks who'd miss a pass, and when they came off the field I'd ask them, "What did you see?" Sometimes they couldn't tell me what they saw. I'd say, "Well, if you don't know what you saw or what to look for, or if you aren't looking for what we talked about in practice, how in the world are you going to be a successful quarterback?" Successfully looking, seeing, listening, and hearing are very important.

There are all kinds of things that you want to look for. For example, you go back to pass and there's a receiver coming across the middle about six or seven yards off the line of scrimmage. Obviously, you need to be looking for

him, but you also need to look behind him to
make sure he's got separation from his defenders, and you need to look ahead of him to make
sure no one is entering his path. That's just a
small example of how important looking is.
Seeing also plays an important role in reading
defenses. To young kids, reading defenses may
not be important, but certainly by junior high or
high school, potential quarterbacks need to
know that they have to look downfield and
discern the defense's intentions.

The biggest hindrance to good field vision
for a quarterback is big, tall offensive and
defensive linemen. Imagine standing at the
edge of a forest of tall trees. If you stand right
up against one tree and look directly at it,
you'll miss the whole forest. In order to really
see the other trees you have to "see through"
the ones directly in front of you. What makes
being a quarterback so hard is that all of the
"trees" (or players) in your forest are moving.
Many times you're only going to get small
glimpses of what's unfolding downfield. You
must have the discipline to be able to "look
through" the defense to "see" the offense. It's
not easy to do.

Usually when a quarterback drops back his
head is on a swivel. He starts looking around,
and all he sees is the other team and the backs
of his linemen. This is why very young quarterbacks have a tendency to leave the pocket too
early. When they're in the pocket they can't see
through the linemen. The coach says, "Well, the

guy was wide open. Why didn't you throw it?"
and the kid answers, "I didn't see him."
Eventually all good quarterbacks learn to trust
their protection and place their focus downfield.

If you are on a team that doesn't give you
great pass protection, you have to get past that.
You have to believe on every snap that they are
going to do the job. If you lose faith in your
offensive line you'll never be able to play to
your potential, because you'll be preoccupied
with the pass rush. That's where peripheral
vision comes in again. By peripheral I don't
just mean being able to see side-to-side, I also
mean being able to look downfield and see
what's happening in an area. No quarterback
can see the whole field from the pocket. But he
needs to know what to look for, and if one
receiver is covered, he must move on to the
next one. He looks at an area and sees the picture in his mind.

When players are watching a game film, a
coach can freeze it—stop the picture—and he
can look and say at that very moment, "This is
what's happening and this is where everybody
is." As a quarterback your mind has to operate
that same way. Once I was coaching with a certain NFL team (I won't say which one) and the
quarterback was having a real tough time getting the ball off. After a particularly dismal
series he came to the sideline and I asked him
what was wrong. He started telling me that a
couple of defenders kept breaking through the
pass protection. He was even able to tell me

what their numbers were. Right then I knew
that the problem was not only our pass protection, it was our quarterback. If a quarterback is
able to tell you the numbers on the defenders'
jerseys, then he's no longer focusing down the
field, he's focusing on the rush.

Think about a quarterback like **Doug Flutie**.
As short as he is, how does he manage? He's
got exceptional peripheral vision, and he's
learned to look through the people in front of
him. Ever notice that he's always moving? That
is not simply a matter of nerves or footwork.
That's vision. He is moving within (and sometimes outside) the pocket in an attempt to see
through the trees.

That's the reason why a quarterback should
have a little bit of movement in the pocket. And
when I say a little I mean a little. When you
start moving three steps to your left or three
steps to your right then you're out of the
pocket. At that point you've created a real
problem for your linemen because they don't
know where you are. So it's just a slight movement of a foot or two that gets you in position
to see beyond the obstacles in front of you.

Sometimes you know a rusher is coming in
on you, but you can't see him. It could be a
hand pulling your jersey or the sound of a
defensive lineman charging at you. Believe it or
not, if you are concentrating downfield you're
more likely to give the rusher the slip than if
you focus directly on him.

One of the criteria I've used in evaluating

quarterbacks coming out of college was whether or not they watch the receivers or the pass rush. I can see this in their game films. Too often you see quarterbacks take off as soon as a defender gets through the pass protection. Some coaches will say, "He has an uncanny ability to get away." My reaction is, "It's easy to get away when all you're watching is the pass rush." In my opinion, a quarterback simply cannot function if he's watching the pass rush.

With great vision you can make great decisions. Jim Zorn, whom I coached with the Seattle Seahawks, had tremendous vision. He was a great scrambler, and when he got out of the pocket he could really hurt you. **Timm Rosenbaugh** of the Arizona Cardinals was another player who had great anticipation and great vision. You don't have to have 20/20 eyesight. Plenty of good quarterbacks have worn contact lenses. You just need to be able to look for things and locate them. A coach can help you with this.

Now let's talk a little bit about good ears. Good ears means listening. It all starts with you and the coaching staff. Whether it's in a team meeting or a discussion with the coach on the sideline as you come off the field, listen to what he's telling you. You may have just got your brain rattled by a defensive end but you must pay attention. The information your coach is giving you may save you from getting your head rattled again.

Not all exchanges of information are blown

by the player. Sometimes coaches blow the opportunity to communicate valuable information to their kids. Instead of being reasonable and constructive, they get upset and tear a kid down emotionally. You may have a few coaches

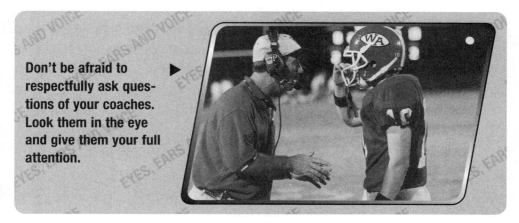

Don't be afraid to respectfully ask questions of your coaches. Look them in the eye and give them your full attention.

in your career who use an in-your-face style. It's still up to you as a player to listen, to show respect. Look your coach in the eye and listen. Respond, too. When your coach asks if you understand something, don't just grunt or walk away. Look him in the eye and say, "Yes, sir" or "Yes, Coach." If you don't understand, say so. He'll gladly go through it with you again. Quarterbacks need to listen to their teammates, too. You're a team leader so they'll be coming to you with a lot of things. But be careful with your teammates, some of them will have their own interests at heart: They want the ball. The one thing a quarterback learns early on is that every receiver is "wide open" on just about every play. From Pop Warner football to the Pro Bowl, receivers tell their quarterbacks, "I was

wide open," or, "I can beat my guy."

Obviously, they're not all open all the time, plus even if they were you can only throw it to one guy at a time. But you still have to show them some respect and listen to them. Let them feel confident, let them think they're always open, it'll make them better receivers.

Listening to your opponents is also important. Once on the field, most people would be surprised at how much chatter is going on. Sure, there's silly stuff, like guys on opposing teams popping off at one another. But there's also a lot of good information flying around a football field. If you're alert, you might pick up a word that means something. Say you're at the line of scrimmage and the player calling the signals for the defense shouts a code word to his teammates. "Rocket, rocket!" Then you notice that every time he shouts that term, his linebackers drop back and play zone. Now you know something very valuable. The same way that a defense tries to pick up repetitive cues from a quarterback, you can pick up the same stuff from them.

I would also strongly suggest that when coaches and quarterbacks are talking on television, listen closely. When you're in a team meeting, take notes. You might be the only guy in the room who's writing things down, but it really comes down to how good you want to be. **How far will you go? What will you do to gain the edge?**

That's eyes and ears, now for the voice. Your

At the line of scrimmage be alert to any signals the defense may be calling. They may tip you off to their plans.

voice is the way you communicate with your players and your coaches. How you use your voice tells them a lot about how confident you are. If you feel confident, I guarantee that your teammates and coaches will feel more confident. We're talking about clarity and about strength—the ability to project your voice clearly and loudly. We're also talking about calmness. When you step into the huddle you want to have a very calm, strong, clear voice. Call the plays very clearly and very plainly. The calmer you are and the more precisely you enunciate the words the more confidence your team is going to have in what you're saying. Plus, and this is important too, they're all going to hear you. It's amazing to me that a quarterback can go into a huddle and call a play, and all ten guys can then go to the line of scrimmage with only nine of them hearing you perfectly, and the other one not even remembering what you said. That's where mistakes happen—guys go offsides or forget the snap count. But speaking clearly, calmly, and confidently in the huddle can eliminate a lot of those mistakes. Understand that in the huddle, while

everyone should be focusing on you and what you're saying, many of your teammates will be distracted. Odds are one of them is thinking, "Oh, my hand is killing me." Another is thinking, "Man, I can't block my guy." But with his voice, the quarterback can calm everybody down. He can call the play in such a way that all of his team-mates leave the huddle thinking, "This sounds like it's going to work." When they think that way, they'll make it work.

**Bart Starr**, the legendary quarterback of the Green Bay Packers during their dynasty years, said that his wife called him Dr. Jekyll and Mr. Hyde because around the house he never raised his voice. He was always very soft spoken and easygoing. But when he stepped on the football field, into the huddle and up to that line of scrimmage, he was like a lion. What he was trying to do was show his teammates that he had confidence. He was trying to reassure them that the play was going to be a great one.

Certainly the line of scrimmage can be a loud place. In junior high and high school you might have to begin dealing with the added noise of marching bands. You're barking out signals and the defense is yelling out things, too. The linebackers are talking back and forth, screaming and hollering. In fact, everybody's screaming and hollering. I have one rule of thumb for overcoming noise with your voice: If your mother or father can hear you from the stands, you're doing fine.

I've taken NFL rookies and put them in the

huddle to call a play. Then I would call them aside and say, "Is that the way you called plays in college?" And they'd say, "Well, yeah." And I'd say, "You want to hear how to call a play?" Then I'd step in the huddle and call it. "Brown right. Edge 31. On two, ON TWO." That's how you call a play. Look your teammates straight in the eye and shout the signals. They'd say, "Well, I don't want to be too loud. They're going to hear it on defense." I'd say "Hear it on defense? Give me a break, your own guys can't hear you!"

There are ways to work on the volume or projection of your voice. At practice, when the quarterbacks and centers are working on the exchange, that's a great time to see how loud you can bark the snap count. At home, go in the backyard and practice your cadence. See if you can get all the dogs in the neighborhood barking in unison.

## *Drills*

### ✓ *1. Voice Drill*

As I mentioned earlier, I have quarterbacks call practice signals in unison. I want my quarterbacks to sound alike. Think about it. The starter gets hurt and has to leave the game. You come in off the bench. Everybody has been listening to him, hearing his voice and his rhythm. Now you come in there and you give them a totally different

rhythm, a totally different voice. What's going to happen? They're going to be jumping offsides. I get my quarterbacks to work in unison together so that everybody has a similar sound or cadence.

Some kids struggle with all this yelling. I've seen pretty good quarterbacks lose their voices. I've always suggested chewing gum. Nervousness makes your mouth dry. So does a lot of yelling. So imagine coming into a huddle and you're nervous already and you've got cottonmouth. You can't even talk. I never went near a football field without chewing gum. I've had quarterbacks that went through two packs a game to keep things going.

### ✓ 2. Eyes Drill

Now what's a good drill for eyes? You can have three or four players stand down the field 15 yards apart and 20 yards down the field. Another guy stands behind the quarterback. The guy behind the quarterback points to the one of the guys downfield. That guy lifts his hand up slightly, not even to his shoulder. The quarterback sets up, then delivers the ball to that player. Now, that's not exactly what happens on the field, but the drill forces the quarterback to get his peripheral vision working. He's expanding his field of vision. Instead of looking at all four receivers one at a time, this forces him to see all four at once.

Then it's nice to put one receiver short, one on the sideline and one moved in ten yards, all with their hands in front of their chest. Have

the quarterback drop back and throw to the receiver who opens his hands.

Another twist is to put three receivers downfield. Spread them out and deepen the middle receiver. Take a defensive man and put him in front of the middle receiver. If the defender moves left, the quarterback throws right. If the defender moves right, the quarterback throws left. If the defender comes upfield, you throw downfield behind him.

This chapter can really help a young player if he just takes it one little step at a time. You can't do it all on the practice field. You've got to go home and you've got to go in your backyard and get your father or your friends involved. If you do it right, it can be a lot of fun. Everybody can dream up their own drills. And that makes it even more fun.

## TIPS

- Your eyes are a vital tool
- See "through" defenders
- Be aware of the pocket
- Focus downfield, not on the pass rush
- Listen
- Lead with your voice
- Don't be bashful, bark out the signals

# ChapterSeven

# The Field General

## Leadership in the Huddle

The huddle is really the heart of an offense. If your team is sloppy and disorganized in the huddle then they going to play sloppy football. If they are snappy and sharp going in and coming out of the huddle it will lead to a quick and aggressive style of play.

The key to a good huddle is limited conversation. The only guy who's authorized to talk in the huddle is the signal caller, the quarterback. Why? The less chatter there is in the huddle, the better the chance there is of everyone listening and understanding the play. Now, most huddles, even on well-organized teams, are not that simple. Some players will have a kind word for a teammate. Sometimes, a player will offer an apology for a penalty or a dropped pass. And then the quarterback himself may add a few words. Every huddle is not as cut and dried as, "Green right, X-34, Quick Pass on 2." You might walk in the huddle and say, "Alright you guys, we've got to have this one. We know they're going to blitz us so let's be particularly tight on our pass blocking."

The quarterback can sometimes provide encouragement, but don't overdo it. It's okay to start off by saying, "Hey, great catch Jimmy." A little credit scattered around isn't bad either. Positive things like, "Jim, you're

**Huddle Command
Track 20**

doing a great job of holding off that guy." Then you go on with the play. But don't get into making speeches. You've got to get in and get out of the huddle so you don't draw a delay-of-game penalty. One thing that makes a football team go is that in-and-out-of-the-huddle time. You get in the huddle, get the play called correctly, and get your teammates out of the huddle and up to the line of scrimmage. That sets the rhythm for the game. You get into a rhythm and then you start feeling confident. This is a great way for the quarterback to take control. You can really tell whether or not a quarterback has confidence once he steps into that huddle and starts calling signals. You can just tell by his demeanor and how he handles himself.

You can practice an imaginary huddle in your bedroom. Step into the imaginary huddle and practice looking at everybody. It may sound silly, but practicing is very important before being in your first real huddle.

So starting that huddle is extremely important. Get into a position where you're comfortable and you can look your teammates straight in the eye. Maybe you want to get down on one knee and look up. You may have a huddle that's round and you're leaning into it. Or you may have a stand-up huddle where they're all in lines and you're in front of them. No matter what kind of huddle you have, you need to be able to make eye contact with your teammates. Move your head around so you're speaking to all of your players, making eye contact with

each one. Call the play loud and clear, and repeat the snap count. The huddle finishes with the quarterback saying "Ready," and the whole team responds, "Break!" with a simultaneous clap of the hands. The key is to get them in and out, up to the line of scrimmage and ready to

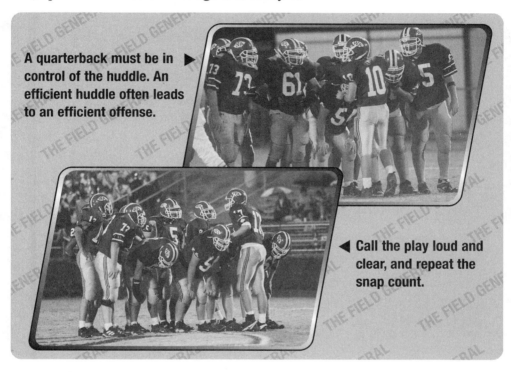

A quarterback must be in ▶ control of the huddle. An efficient huddle often leads to an efficient offense.

◀ Call the play loud and clear, and repeat the snap count.

go. (NOTE: If you're having trouble making yourself heard, make sure that your mouthpiece is removed while you call the play and then re-insert it before you get to the line of scrim-mage. Again, I recommend chewing gum. It will help keep your mouth moist so that you can speak more clearly.)

As a quarterback and team leader, you should always move quickly from the huddle to

the line of scrimmage and set the tempo for everyone else. No one on a football team should ever walk to the line of scrimmage.

As the team approaches the line of scrimmage each player should be repeating the snap count in his mind. Why so much emphasis on the snap count? Because everyone is so concerned with the responsibilities for the called play that they're likely to miss or forget the count. An offside penalty can really hurt, especially if it comes at a critical time in the game.

It's extremely important for the quarterback to control the huddle and to clamp down on those who talk too much. A quarterback needs to let his players know that he simply is not going to allow this. The worst thing that can happen is a quarterback losing control of the huddle.

## Line of Scrimmage

We've already talked about vision and looking down the field. But wherever you do end up looking, learn something from what you're looking at. If you really want to have some fun, stare down the middle linebacker. I remember playing against the Chicago Bears and **Dick Butkus** would be across the line of scrimmage just foaming at the mouth and growling and grumbling. I had fun just looking right at him.

As a quarterback, you're always better off concentrating on the secondary. Don't waste your time worrying about defensive tackles and defensive ends. Look and see where the safeties and the corners are lined up. I bring this up

because even good quarterbacks can get into bad habits. They often make one of two mistakes. They walk up to the line of scrimmage and either unconsciously stare at the spot where the ball is going to be thrown or, thinking that they don't want to tip off the defense, they look the other way. Trust me, it doesn't take a defense very long to figure out either tendency.

**Up to this point, much of the information in this chapter has been for the experienced quarterback. If you're about to play your first game, I suggest concentrating mainly on the tips below.**

## TIPS

- Manage the huddle
- Speak slowly, clearly, and confidently
- Move quickly to the line of scrimmage
- Know what your eyes are "saying"

## Voice and Cadence

Get out in your backyard, put a chair out, and pretend it's the center. Walk up to it, put your hands underneath, and bark out the signals loud enough for your neighbors two houses over to hear. I know that sounds silly, but when it's really happening in a game or practice, it will

be much easier. Sometimes, inexperienced quarterbacks feel self-conscious. But if you've practiced it already you'll be used to it, and you'll be fine.

I've run some football camps, and I've coached quarterbacks who are just starting out. I'll be standing right next to them or right behind them, and I can hardly hear the snap count. I usually take them aside and say, "Are you afraid you're going to hurt someone's feelings by being too loud? Are you going to bother somebody?" The fact is that in the entire history of football, there's never been a quarterback who called his signals too loudly.

## Dealing with Coaches and Teammates

When your coach talks to you, look him straight in the eye. Don't be looking at the ground or up at the sky. Look him straight in the eye and listen. Let him know that you're listening and tell him when you understand something (it's just as important to tell him when you don't understand something). There's not a better feeling for a coach than to be looking at a player and have him looking you straight in the eye, acknowledging that he's listening to you. For a coach there's nothing worse than talking to a player, trying to help him, and he's looking everywhere but at you. As a player, do yourself a favor. Look your coaches straight in the eye and listen.

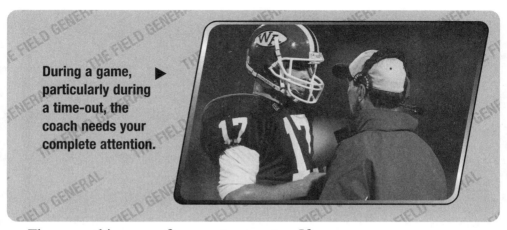

During a game, ▶ particularly during a time-out, the coach needs your complete attention.

The same thing goes for your teammates. If one of your teammates comes up to you with a question or comment, look him straight in the eye. Likewise, if you've got something to say to a teammate, again, look him straight in the eye. This goes for positive and negative stuff. When your teammate scores a touchdown, look him in the eye and tell him "Great job." If a teammate is talking too much in the huddle, look him in the eye and be firm—not bossy, but firm. One of the biggest headaches that quarterbacks face is that after just about every pass every one of the receivers who didn't get the ball will complain that they were wide open on the play. The best way to handle this is to let them know that you're looking for them. Tell them to be patient, to stick with you and to understand that the play and the defense dictate where the quarterback looks on a given play. And encourage them to keep getting open. Drew Bledsoe explains it well on the DVD. If you want to earn the respect of your coaches and team-

mates, dish out as much credit as you can and accept as much blame as you can.

There is a fine line between what a quarterback can say to his teammates and what he should leave to the coaches. One thing I never tolerated as a coach was having my quarterback chew out his own teammates. Every time I caught a quarterback doing that I pulled him aside and reminded him, "Hey, I'm the coach." First of all, it's bad leadership. Second of all, the next time he throws an interception he's not going to want his teammates getting in his face. That's what a team is all about, helping each other, not ragging on each other. There's nothing wrong with trying to get on the same page with your teammates, and I've always encouraged that. Say a receiver is supposed to cut out on a certain play, but instead he cut in. In that case, there's nothing wrong with a quarterback going over and saying, "You know, I think you were supposed to cut out on that one." It's okay to talk it over in a constructive way. But to go over and chew him out because he went the wrong direction, what good is that going to do? It's not productive at all. In fact, it's destructive. A good coach will always put a stop to that kind of behavior.

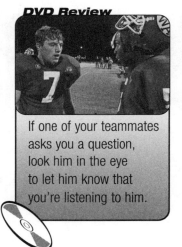

**DVD Review**

If one of your teammates asks you a question, look him in the eye to let him know that you're listening to him.

**TIPS**

- Look coaches in the eye
- Listen and respond
- Offer credit, accept blame

# ChapterEight

# The Elements of Leadership

## Qualifications of the Heart

I think this is extremely important, not only in football but in anything you may do in life. You've got to be honest and look in the mirror and say to yourself: Is this what I really

want to do, or is someone telling me to do this? Am I doing this because I enjoy it or because it might help me meet girls or make me more popular? All that is phony stuff. You've got to want to play football for your own satisfaction, or you're not going to succeed. Do you have the determination and the dedication to succeed?

If the answer to these questions is no, forget it. No big deal, just move on to a different sport or a different activity. I've seen guys who had all the football talent in the world and just weren't dedicated. They found something else. That's what separates the player from the pretender—caring. It's more important than talent. Give me eleven dedicated guys, and I'll take them anytime over eleven guys who have size and speed but don't give a hoot.

What does dedication mean? It means going the extra mile because you care. You're sitting there taking notes while everybody's looking out the window. You're there five minutes before the team meeting starts, you've already got your notebook out and you're getting ready to review. You go to the coach and ask if there's anything you can take home to read. Instead of

going home and watching television you get your schoolwork done.

**Larry Centers** is one of the most dedicated players I've ever been around. He played for the Arizona Cardinals when I was coaching there. He didn't play high school football until his senior year because his mother wouldn't let him. His mother raised him in a little town outside Longview, Texas. And she made him play the violin. Finally, in his senior year, somebody talked her into letting him play football. He went to college on a partial scholarship and did very well. So I went and worked him out and watched him play. I was absolutely convinced that he could play professional football. What I liked most about him was his dedication. He was so gung-ho, and he wanted to be successful. We drafted him in the fifth round, but afterwards he kept getting hurt. He was going to start a game his rookie year, and two days before the game he cracked his foot. After two years of on-and-off injuries, the Cardinals were going to let Larry go. I went to the head coach, Joe Bugel, and changed his mind. He listened and the rest is literally NFL history. Larry is now the NFL's all time leading receiver among running backs.

I went to bat for Larry because Larry always went the extra mile. Was his skill enough to carry him? I don't think so. Frankly, I don't think he would have had a chance to play in the NFL based on skill alone. Here's a guy who didn't get to play football until very late in his career. He had to be dedicated to go to college and make the team and stay in school. Then when he came to the Cardinals it was a constant uphill battle for him because nobody really believed in him but me and his backfield coach, **Bobby Hammond.** If you were to take that same kid and go back and look at him in college, high school, and junior high, I'll bet you anything he was dedicated back in those days, too. And that's probably what kept him going on through the years. There's no substitute for dedication and hard work.

## Courage

It doesn't take long to look out over a football field and pick out the five most courageous players. Courage comes from the heart and shows on the field. A friend recently told me about a high school kid who played nose guard. He was small and quick but he didn't have a lot of beef on him. He came up against a guy who was playing center for the other team, all-State, and headed to a Division I school on scholarship. Anyway, the defensive coach told the nose guard, "Look, you're going to have a tough day today. You know there's not much we can do. This guy outweighs you by 100 pounds, but we need you to keep him busy. Do the best you can." Well, that nose guard got his head handed to him that day. And his team ended up losing, but only by a touchdown, to a heavy favorite. The losing coach gave the game ball to this little nose guard and said, "Your man made a lot of plays today. But he would

have made 50 more if you hadn't been such a rascal with him. Thank you and congratulations." This kid was getting slapped upside down, spun around, knocked over, trampled on, and he'd just put his chin strap on and step right up against this guy on every play. That's being courageous.

My nephew, John Herring, was legally blind by the time he got to high school. He was about 6-foot 3-inches and weighed about 240 pounds. And he played football. The guy who played next to him on the defensive line held hands with him to guide him onto the field. When John got down in his stance his teammates would hold his hands to help him line up. You know what? Nobody ran through his area. He tackled every-body, including his own guys. You just didn't get near John unless you were ready to go down. John was voted the most courageous player in the city of Tulsa his senior year. Talk about dedi-cation and courage. He's my hero.

Dedication is a state of mind, and it's related to attitude. In addition to doing all the things that a dedicated person does, those things need to be performed with a positive, upbeat attitude if you're going to inspire yourself or others. The more dedicated you are the more likely you are to be upbeat. Now everybody gets into moods, and that's certainly understandable. Not every single player wants to go to practice every sin-gle day. But the dedicated players—the ones with the positive attitudes—overcome that, and they can help others overcome it too. Inside you might be feeling the same as your teammates who moan and groan through practice, but you're a quarterback. Your teammates are looking to you for a signal. You've got to pick everybody up. And if you can do it at practice, you can do it on the field. And if you can do it on the field, you can do it off the field, too.

Think of the sergeant who leads his soldiers into battle. Would he rather be drinking cold sodas by the pool? Sure. But what does he do? He says, "Guys, right now we've got to do the things that we've been trained to do." The coach has to have an upbeat attitude, and that filters down to the quarterback. But it only filters down if the quarterback wants to accept the responsibility of playing this position, with the knowledge that all eyes are on you. If you go out there and start slopping around (here we go with that word sloppy again) your teammates will all go out and slop around with you.

Let's talk about guys who had real good attitudes. Joe Theismann was amazing. When he stepped into the huddle there was a "bang"—a shot of positive momentum. He's one of those guys who made the energy level of everyone around him rise, just for being in his presence. I mention Theismann because he's the perfect example of a guy who accomplished a lot because of his personality. He was overflowing with confidence and overflowing with upbeat attitude. Timm Rosenbaugh was also that way. When he stepped into the huddle, you just wanted to get to work. **Roger Staubach** was also very upbeat, and that was a great plus for him.

# *Are You Coachable?*

Are you coachable? That's a tough question because you've got your opinion and the coach has his. It's a two-way street, of course, but you're the one who's playing for him. And you have to accept constructive criticism. As a player, how do you distinguish between someone who's just criticizing you to tear you down and someone whose criticism is trying to build you up? Compassion. That is, we need to make sure that genuine concern for the player and understanding of his situation are mixed in with our instructions. If a coach shows some compassion, kids will listen more closely. We had a coach in junior high basketball that we all would have killed to play for. The man hardly said a word, so when he did speak we knew it was straight from his heart. We'd do anything to make this guy happy. When I talk to a player I want to be able to give them that same feeling. If the players believe in a coach, they're going to do great things, things that they're really not even capable of doing. So that upbeat attitude works hand in hand with dedication, and dedication works hand in hand with compassion.

So how do you know if you're coachable? Ask yourself a few questions: Am I really learning or do I just go out to the practice field and go through the same old motions every day? Am I listening? Do I hear my coaches; that is, do I listen to what they say and act on it or do I just shut them out? Am I improving?

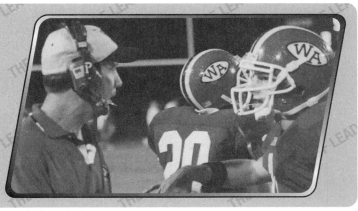

As a coach I've always felt that constructive, compassionate criticism worked better than berating or demeaning a player.

Improvement in play tells a lot. It says you care, it says you're listening, and it also says that there is some talent inside you that's being tapped. Am I looking at it from both sides? If I'm clashing with my coach, why is that? Is it partly my fault, my attitude, my own failure? As an NFL coach I was lucky. I had a lot of very talented and very coachable players. Dave Kreig and Jim Zorn were extremely coachable, and Aikman was very coachable, too. This was because they all wanted to hear what their coaches had to say.

I've also had some players who were difficult to coach. Chris Chandler was extremely coachable only after we got past a certain point in our relationship. With Chris it was kind of like breaking a horse. He was very independent-minded. We finally had a meeting, and he realized that I knew what I was talking about. He became extremely coachable from that point on, and his career skyrocketed. Once he accepted that someone knew more about football than

he did, his career went straight up. We were able to replace conceit with confidence. Conceit and confidence may look very similar from the outside. However, conceit is a more self-centered way of thinking. Having confidence is knowing in your heart that you can get it done—believing in yourself, your players, your coaches, and teammates, and them all believing in you and knowing that WE are going to do this. It's not what "I" did today; it's what "we" did today that's important. If I'm using the word "I" all the time, then I'm thinking about me. That's conceited and selfish. The more you think about yourself the more trouble you're going to have in a team sport. It may be true that you're the best player and it may be true that without you they would just be an average team, but once you become an "I" you're not really a part of a team.

Now we know that confidence is better than conceit or cockiness, but what about over-confidence? Too much confidence can be a problem, too. When I was playing and coaching I used to love playing overly-confident teams. Think about the 2002 Super Bowl. How did St. Louis, the premier team in the NFL, lose to the New England Patriots, a team that barely made it through the playoffs? Did the Rams show up feeling overly-confident or did they go out there with confidence and just have some bad luck? Could it be that New England went into the game with so much confidence and so much nothing-to-lose attitude that it carried them to victory?

## *Are You a Competitor?*

Do you like a challenge? Do you enjoy the battle as much as the spoils? Do you have confidence in your ability and enjoy matching your ability against that of others? If you answered yes, you're probably a competitor. And that's a good thing, because I don't think you can play quarterback unless you're really a competitor. A competitor needs confidence (the right kind, in the right amounts). How do you build confidence? Practice. If properly coached, the more you work at something the better you will become. Some people don't want to practice, they don't want to pay the price for excellence. But the old saying is still true today: Practice makes perfect. I've competed with guys who do a lot of talking but don't prepare. Their mouth is bigger than their ability. That kind of talk is not confidence. It's bravado or false confidence, and it almost never prevails over the quiet confidence that comes from practice and preparation. True, you're only as good as you think you are, but you have to prepare in order to really feel that strength inside you.

Have you ever seen the basketball movie "Hoosiers?" Remember when the game is on the line and the coach calls a play for one kid and all the kids stare back at the coach with blank disappointment? The coach asks, "What's wrong?" and the other kids say, "Jimmy can make it." And the coach says, "Can you Jimmy?" And Jimmy goes, "Yeah." Jimmy goes on to make the shot and his team wins the State

Championship. Jimmy had quiet confidence. That's believing and knowing that your guys around you believe in you. All you need to do is rise to the occasion. That comes from being confident—not cocky—based on hours of practice, preparation, and dedication.

Who are the real competitors at the quarterback position in the NFL these days? Brett Favre is a great competitor. Kurt Warner is also a heck of a competitor. I know that from coaching him back when he was a third-string quarterback with St. Louis. He'd go against the first team defense in practice, and he'd tear them apart. Doug Williams was also a heck of a competitor. I remember him getting off the turf near the end of the first quarter in Super Bowl XXII. We were down 10-0 and he was hurt. He limped off the field, and I got him on the phone from the booth and I said, "Doug, are you alright?" He said, "I hurt my knee." I said, "Doug, are you good to play?" And he said, "Jerry, I would play if I didn't have any legs. I'm gonna win this game for us." I said, "Okay, good. Then the very next time you catch **Ricky Sanders** or **Art Monk** or **Gary Clark** one-on-one pressed against that corner on the right side, take the shot." On the very first play of the second quarter, he threw an 80-yard touchdown pass. At the time it was the longest pass in Super Bowl history.

# *Losing with Grace*

No matter how good you are, no matter how much you practice or how much confidence you amass, you are going to lose games. Some of those losses will be embarrassing blowouts, others will be last-minute defeats. When the game is over, if you find yourself on the losing team, treat your opponent with respect. That's being a gracious loser. Gracious losing is not just saying, "Well, everything is okay. We'll win the next one." I'm talking about giving your opponent the credit and respect he deserves. Have the class to say to the players and coaches on the other team, "You guys played well, congratulations." No excuses. In your mind you may be saying, "I'll get you another time," but that's not what you should say. You should treat your opponent with respect. Even in the NFL—when the hardest-fought games are over—the players go out and shake each other's hands. You may have noticed that a lot of them even gather in prayer in the middle of the field. I think that's great.

**DVD Review**

Exhibit good sportsmanship throughout the game, but particularly afterwards. It's the right thing to do. It also tames your opponents for the rematch.

On the flip side you need to be a gracious winner, too. There are players who don't know how to win. They may get in people's faces. You don't have to do that. If you won, you won. You don't have to boast about it or taunt the other team. That's classless. You're better off just saying to the losing team, "Good job, we had to reach down and get something today. You guys really pushed us." Not only is that the

classy thing to do, but I'll tell you something: Losing teams remember how you handle victory. Be obnoxious about it, rub their faces in it, and all you're doing is psyching them up for next year's game. They're already going to spend the next year figuring out how to beat you. Don't give them any extra incentive.

Coach Landry was a very, very gracious loser—a quiet, classy competitor. After a loss, he didn't say a whole lot. He didn't rant and rave, nor did he make excuses. He would sit us all down, and he would talk about the game and where we made our mistakes. "We're going to get this corrected," he would say. And then he would remind us that "the measure of a great team is what they do after they get knocked down. How are we going to respond to this? I'll tell you how: We're going to work. And we're going to get back to where we need to be." Even as a fierce competitor, you too can be just as courageous, just as gracious, and just as thoughtful.

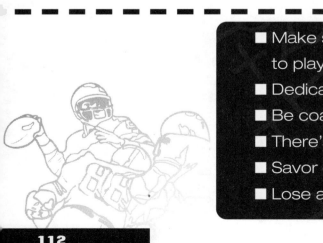

**TIPS**

- Make sure you want to play football
- Dedicate yourself
- Be coachable
- There's no "I" in "TEAM"
- Savor competition
- Lose and win graciously

# ChapterNine
# *The Bus Ride*

## *Fighting the Demons*

I don't know how many team bus rides I've been on in my career. Thinking back to Pop Warner, junior high, high school, college, and pro ball, I've been on more than I care to count. They all have one thing in common: At some point while you're making that trip, the demons inevitably enter the picture. They have one purpose: To undermine your confidence and fill you with negative thoughts. They get you to question your ability. Can you really lead a team? Can you pass well? Are you physically tough enough? These kinds of questions swirl through the mind of every player on your team (and the other team as well).

When I was a kid there was this one particular street our bus used to take. It was a pretty busy street with a lot of houses on it. Throughout high school, I'd get on the bus for the ride to the stadium. I'd see these happy people sitting on their porches. They'd eaten supper and now they were out on their porches visiting one another. I was on my way to play in a football game but wishing that I was just sitting on that porch. How nice it would be, I imagined, if I didn't have to think about anything but sitting on that porch. I wouldn't have all the responsibility of trying to lead a team.

But as the blocks went by and I got closer and closer to the stadium, I would inevitably have a change of heart. I'd start talking to myself, saying, "Boy what a great opportunity. How many people get the opportunity to play quarterback? I've got the chance. I've worked hard, I've prepared

myself." And by the time I got to the stadium I'd be thinking about those poor people sitting on the porch and thinking, "I sure am glad I'm not sitting on that porch. They don't get to do this." By the time we were on the field I was ready to go.

The point is that it's perfectly normal for a young football player to experience these conflicting emotions before a game. I've seen it at all levels. Even in the NFL, guys go a little crazy before a game. Some love to have loud music around them. Others don't want to hear anything. Some of them sit at their lockers and read a book. They're doing everything they can to psych themselves up and get ready to play.

Most of the quarterbacks that I worked with stayed to themselves before games. A lot of guys like hanging out in the training room. But they're all fighting the same thing—the demons. Find what works for you. If you're wound a little tight before a game, find something that calms you down a little bit. If you're like some of the guys whose nervousness actually translates into sleepiness, take a nap. In the end, remember, it's a game. Too many kids get wrapped up in, Am I going to fail or succeed? Hey, it's fun. You're out there on the field running around. What could be better than that? You're healthy and free and competing in the sport you love. God Bless America.

## The Locker Room

Remember, coaches rarely see you outside of a school or football setting. They can only judge you by what they see when they are with you. Other than the effort you give on the field, the thing they see the most is your locker. Keep a clean, neat locker. Know where your shoes are. Don't wander around wondering where you left your helmet. Know where it is at all times. Don't be going and getting stuff out of someone else's locker, and don't be playing games such as hiding stuff from your teammates. The biggest waste of time is roughhousing. You're more likely to sustain an injury while goofing off in the locker room than you are while playing a football game. Just be mature. It doesn't matter how old you are. When you're in that locker room act like a man. Respect yourself, respect other people, and respect their property. Just as there are leaders on the field, a team needs leaders in the locker room.

## Practice

On the practice field a lot of things go wrong. People will make mistakes. People will get tired and edgy. You will too. But if you ever want to be seen as a leader, not only by your coaches but also by your teammates, don't ever be the one that's sitting around telling everybody how tired you are. Don't allow yourself to fall into that trap. Why? Because when a true

As a quarterback, set an example by practicing to be the best.

If your teammates see you working hard, they will respect you as a leader.

leader whines, he makes it okay for everybody else to do the same thing. Complainers love company. They're just begging for people to sympathize with their exhaustion and cut them some slack. If the team leader doesn't give in, odds are the team won't either. A good coach can go a long way toward preventing this problem. He needs to know how to be enthusiastic enough to pick people up during a lackluster practice or a bad game. But if he's standing around with his hands in his pockets looking like he's about to fall asleep, that's exactly what the players are going to do. That's when a team leader is really needed.

# The Week

One thing that I always try to do and I always tell my quarterbacks is, "Even if you're not the greatest athlete—you're not the quickest, you're not the fastest, you're not this or that—still try to be out in front. When you're doing drills try to do the drills the best. In other words, compete. Try to set an example. Personally, I could never outrun anybody, but every time we ran wind sprints I was always trying to be out front. I got out-run a lot of the time, but I was always trying. I would be embarrassed if I brought up the rear. I might have been the slowest, but I'll be darned if I was going to finish last. That's just a matter of pride. That's also showing everybody else that you have pride and showing everybody that you're trying to be a leader. You go through a drill and you try to be the best just to set an example. Believe me, the coaches notice things like that. So do your teammates.

# Game Day Preparation

What are you going to eat on game day? Are you eating the right things? You need to check with your coach, your parents, or whoever is taking care of you. My father always had a certain thing for me to eat at a certain time. In pro ball you have a pre-game meal—the players are all there, and they each have certain diets. After your meal, you might go over your notes or go over your plays. You might ask some questions

about responsibilities and adjustments made over the last week. You don't want to drive people crazy but offer little refreshers: "Just remember about halfway through the second quarter, Coach said we're going to run a reverse. So let's make sure that we do a good job with the hand-off."

## Warming Up

**Pre-game is not THE game. Go easy in your pre-kickoff warm-ups.**

When your team takes the field for calisthenics, a lot of things will start going through your mind. What did the coach say about that? I've got to remember that I can pick up that key by looking at that safety. Occasionally your mind may drift off and you're thinking about something else. That's okay. When you're on the field and you're loosening up, you don't have to be totally keyed in. Sometimes you need to relax and just get yourself loose and stretched. If you watch a big-time college program or NFL pre-game routine, you'll often see a coach having non-football discussions with a few of his guys. From that point, it's a slow build-up. "Warm Up" is sort of an odd term for the process. Sure, the point is to warm up your muscles and to increase your flexibility, but rather than warming up, I see the process almost as one of "chilling" down. A pre-game routine should allow you a chance to relax a little bit and eliminate that nervous feeling in your stomach.

As a coach, you always have a pre-game regimen, and it rarely varies. The first 10 minutes we're going to do this, the next 10 minutes we're going to do that. But even a good player can get over-hyper. The key to warm ups is not overdoing it. Don't play the game before the game.

## The Sideline

Not all football games are won on the field. Many of them are won in the coaches' offices during the week as they map out the game plan.

Many games are also won on the sidelines. Sure, that's where coaches make their adjustments, but that's also where most of the team is at any given moment in a game. How does a quarterback behave on the sideline when he's not playing or when the defense is on the field? First, you take care of your own business. Get a little water—good hydration is not only vital to your health but is also one of the most important advantages an athlete can have. Then make sure you check in with your coach. Let him know if you see some problems or opportunities unfolding on the field. Stay alert. Stay informed. And remember, the defense needs your support. Cheer them just as they've been cheering you. If you're not the starting quarterback you need to watch and "play the game" from the sideline. Watch what the two teams are doing, particularly the defense, and plan what you would be doing if you were in the game.

## The Off-Season

It's January. Spring practice doesn't start for another three or four months. What can you do on your own or with friends to improve your skills? Are you just going to watch television or are you going to realize that this is a great opportunity to improve? Go out and throw the football with friends. Assess your weaknesses. Maybe throughout the last season you had a hard time getting comfortable in the pocket. Set up something in your backyard where you practice getting into and staying in the pocket. In other words, football is not just a fall sport. For committed players, it's a year-round investment of time.

You'd be amazed at what a few months of hard work can accomplish. As a coach I used to spend a lot of time with my quarterbacks during the off-season. With some of them that time lasted throughout the entire off-season, maybe three or four sessions a week. They'd come in for an hour-and-a-half inside and then maybe an hour or so on the field. I did that with a bunch of different guys: Jim Zorn, Dave Krieg, Timm Rosenbaugh. I also did it with **Steve McNair** in Houston (before the Oilers became the Tennessee Titans). We spent four days a week doing an hour in the classroom teaching him how to read coverages. We studied plays and patterns, and then we'd go out on the field. I would try to recruit a couple of receivers to come help out. That off-season was a big jump in Steve's abilities.

Dave Krieg probably had one of the most remarkable off-season transitions I've ever seen. Dave really didn't have much football background. He graduated from a small college, and he was a real longshot to play in the NFL. But he got the opportunity, and he made the team his first year. Even so, because his background was so limited, he was really quite far behind the other players. However, he had undeniable talent.

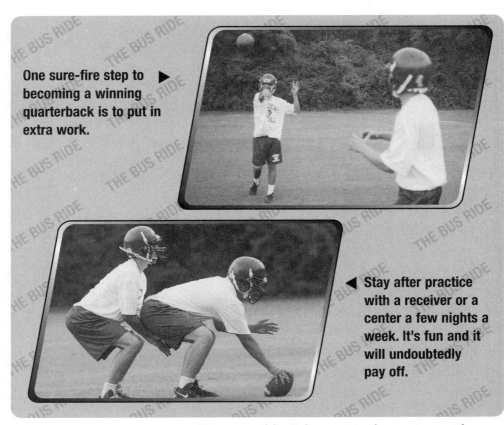

One sure-fire step to ▶
becoming a winning
quarterback is to put in
extra work.

◀ Stay after practice
with a receiver or a
center a few nights a
week. It's fun and it
will undoubtedly
pay off.

We started in February, and we got together three times a week—Monday, Wednesday and Friday. We'd spend a couple hours in the meeting room, and then later as the off-season went by we'd go out and work on the field. I'd tell him about a defensive scheme or a play. We'd talk about it, he'd take notes, and then the next day I would test him. He was a poor student for a while, but as time went by he got a little better and a little better.

One day I'm sitting there after we'd been doing this 'school' for quite a while, and he said, "Jerry, the light bulb just went on!" He said he'd been listening but hadn't really been able to figure it out. Sure enough, he went from making grades of 50 to 60 percent on his tests to grades of 90 percent or higher.

About the same thing happened with another NFL quarterback, Timm Rosenbaugh. The very first time I gave him a test it was the biggest mess you've ever seen. It was absolutely awful.

"Yeah," he'd say, "I never did like taking tests." So one day he turns his paper in and walks out. I look at it and knowing that I use a red pen to correct the tests, he'd written all his answers with a big, thick red pen so that I couldn't correct it. He comes back the next day and I tell him, "This is the biggest piece of crud I have ever read in my life. I don't think you want to play pro football. What's the problem?"

He said "Well, I just don't think all this is important." I said, "Until you see that this is important you're never going to be a player." And slowly he began to understand. He began to prepare, he worked harder, he started to become a student of the game. Timm turned out to be one of the smartest quarterbacks I ever worked with. Within four months he did a total turnaround. He is now the offensive coordinator at Eastern Washington University and absolutely loves football. He's teaching his quarterbacks all the same stuff—tests and all—that I taught him.

This could happen to a kid in grade school, junior high, or high school. Once you make up your mind to make a commitment to something (it might not even be sports), good things are going to happen. You can make tremendous progress during the off-season.

## TIPS

- Nervousness is natural
- Be a leader in the locker room and in practice
- Don't overdo your pre-game routine
- Be alert and engaged on the sideline
- Make the most of the off-season

# ChapterTen

# *The Edge*

## *Seven Steps to Becoming a Winning Quarterback*

**T**he edge. What is it? It's that hard-to-define element that separates winners from losers, quitters from fighters, and successful people from underachievers. The edge has very little to do with talent. Sure, those with enormous natural talent can go a long way. But very few people have that kind of gift. Odds are you do not have it—yet. That's okay, because the way for you to succeed as a quarterback, and ultimately as a person, is to seek that intangible edge.

In looking back over my 40 years in football—33 of them as a player or coach in the NFL—I've found that there are seven ways to get the edge. Here they are:

### *1. Practice Away from the Game*

Quarterbacks have a real knack for working together. I know that through-out my career the guys that I had the most success working out with were other quarterbacks. That's where I developed my confidence and a lot of my skills. I could do it over and over and over and over again. I could mess up dozens of times, and there would be no one there to hear it or see it and I could do it all over again. One of my best friends right now is the guy I had to beat out in high school. We spent an entire summer preparing to compete against each other, and as bad as we each wanted it, it was like,

"Well, whoever plays, plays. But let's make ourselves better." That was great.

### 2. Listen to the Correct Voices

A youngster, quarterback or not, hears a lot of voices. They pop up when you and your buddies step out of the movie theater and a few of the guys want to go do something that you know you shouldn't do. It could be driving around in a car and someone suggests doing something you know is wrong. You might have a friend on the team who doesn't like the coach and is saying things to damage the coach's reputation. Those are the kinds of things you don't want to waste your time listening to. Those are the wrong voices.

Fortunately, there are good voices, too. Some guys may want to have some healthy fun—grab a pizza, go swimming, go to the gym—listen to those voices. Listen to your coaches. Trust me, they know what they're talking about. Most of all, listen to your parents. No one cares about you and your health and welfare more than they do.

While we're on the topic of listening: As a quarterback you're going to get advice from everybody in town on what's going wrong with the team or what you ought to be doing. Just tell them you are behind your coach. Parents, teachers, and coaches are a pretty good place to start.

## 3. Stay in Top Physical Condition

This is one of the greatest edges that an athlete can have. If you're in top physical condition you're out front all the time. And when it's the fourth quarter and the game is on the line, you're not sitting there gasping for air, you're fired up. When everybody else gets tired, you'll have the edge. There's an old saying that being out of shape makes cowards of us all, and it's true. You go from being a tiger to a little pussycat because you run out of gas. Do a little **extra running** on your own. Some of the best players I've ever been around are out there doing more after practice, when everybody else is heading for the showers. That little extra goes a long way.

## 4. Improve Your Physical Strength

Work on your leg strength. Work on your arm strength. On one team I coached we used to have a rope that ran through a pulley in the wall. At the other end of the rope were weights that would slide up and down as you moved your arm. Your trainer or coach can give you lots of drills to increase your arm strength. For instance I used to have my players **get down on one knee and throw the ball** without any legs involved and just work on building up that over-the-top motion and strength. Coach Arians offers an excellent once-a-week drill on the DVD. He suggests playing catch with a friend who goes higher and higher up the stands. Put

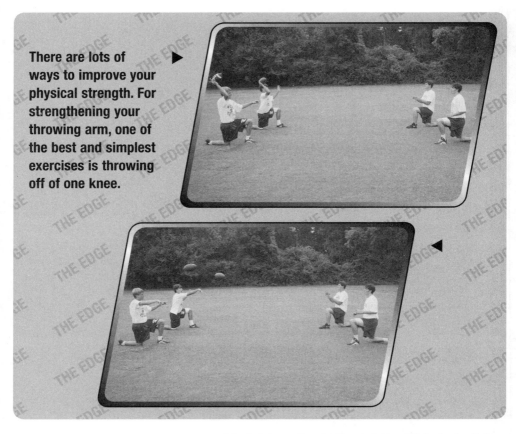

There are lots of ways to improve your physical strength. For strengthening your throwing arm, one of the best and simplest exercises is throwing off of one knee.

good height on the ball, and it will help build arm strength and accuracy. Do curls, presses, bench presses—whatever your trainer and coach suggest. Having good tone throughout your body just keeps you physically strong. I definitely recommend a professionally designed, supervised weight training program for junior high and high school players. Start in junior high, and I think it'll really benefit you. Make sure you get specific supervision from your coach or trainer.

## 5. Have the Mindset to Be the Best

Nurture that burning desire to be the best. What are you going to do today, this week, this month that will make you the best possible player you can be? Focus on that. There's plenty of time to have fun, but make sure you check off your work stuff first. My father was always big on getting work done before play, and I always considered football part of my work, although I also considered it fun.

## 6. Beware of Alcohol, Drugs, and Steroids

I can't even count the number of times I've seen alcohol, drugs, or steroids either ruin a great a career, a great reputation, or both. It isn't worth it. Get high on football; it's a lot more fun.

## 7. Stay in School and Make Good Grades

Less than one percent of all the young men playing high school football in the United States this year will end up making their living playing in the NFL. The other 99 percent will make their living as lawyers, doctors, teachers, truck drivers, etc. All of those jobs require a basic education, and three of the four require advanced studies. Play football because it's fun, and it'll teach you a lot about life. Study hard though too, so you will have choices for the future. Good luck. Give it your best shot, and may God be with you.

# Player and Coach Index

**Troy Aikman, Quarterback**
*College:* UCLA
*Professional Career:* Dallas Cowboys, 1989-2000
*Highlights:* Holds practically all Dallas Cowboys passing records...Three Super Bowl wins (XXVII, XXVIII and XXX)...MVP in Super Bowl XXVII...1991 and 1993 Pro Bowl selection...Joins Joe Montana and Terry Bradshaw as the only QBs to win three Super Bowls...Threw for 32,942 career yards...165 TDs...141 INTs.

**Bruce Arians, Coach**
*College:* Virginia Tech
*Professional Career:* 1975 to 1977, graduate assistant, Virginia Tech; '78-'80, running backs and wide receivers coach, Mississippi State; '81-'82, running backs coach, University of Alabama; '83-'88, head coach, Temple University; '89-'92, running backs coach, Kansas City Chiefs; '93-'95, offensive coordinator, Mississippi State; '96, tight ends coach, New Orleans Saints; '97, offensive coordinator, University of Alabama; '98 – '00, quarterbacks coach, Indianapolis Colts; '01-'02, offensive coordinator, Cleveland Browns
*Highlights:* A 27-year coaching veteran, Arians is in his 10th season in the NFL... three seasons with the Indianapolis Colts as quarterbacks coach... instrumental in the development of Peyton Manning... helped Manning become the only player in NFL history to surpass 3,000 yards passing in each of his first three seasons.

**Drew Bledsoe, Quarterback**
*College:* Washington State
*Professional Career:* New England Patriots, 1993-2001; Buffalo Bills,
2002- present
*Highlights:* Holds NFL season record for most pass attempts: 691...NFL game record for most completions: 45...NFL records for completions, attempts and yards in a game and season...Member of the 2001-02 Super Bowl champion Patriots... No. 1 overall draft pick in 1993.

**Jim Brown, Running Back**
*College:* Syracuse University
*Professional Career:* Cleveland Browns, 1957-65
*Highlights:* Pro Football Hall of Fame inductee...Led NFL in rushing 8 times...All-NFL 8 of his 9 years...NFL MVP in 1958 and 1965...NFL Rookie of the Year in 1957...Nine straight Pro Bowl selections...15,459 combined net career yards...756 points scored...Career average of 5.22 yards per carry.

**Dick Butkus, Linebacker**
*College:* Illinois
*Professional Career:* 1965-73, Chicago Bears
*Highlights:* Pro Football Hall of Fame inductee...22 lifetime interceptions...25 fumble recoveries...All-NFL 7 times...Eight straight Pro Bowl appearances...In first NFL game made 11 unassisted tackles vs. San Francisco...In his rookie year he led the Bears in tackles, interceptions, and fumble recoveries. Averaged 128 tackles and 58 assists per season.

**Larry Centers, Running Back**
*College:* Stephen F. Austin
*Professional Career:* Phoenix Cardinals, 1990-98; Washington Redskins, 1999-2000; Buffalo Bills, 2001-present
*Highlights:* First running back in NFL his-

tory to catch 700 passes…In 1994 led all NFL running backs with 647 receiving yards…Two-time Pro Bowl selection…Ranks ninth all-time in receiving…Cardinals' all-time leader in receptions with 523 (one more than Roy Green)…Holds Washington Redskins' running back record for pass receptions in a season (81)…NFL season record for pass receptions by a running back (101)…Cardinals' Unsung Hero in 1996.

**Chris Chandler, Quarterback**
*College:* University of Washington
*Professional Career:* Indianapolis Colts, 1988-89; Tampa Bay Buccaneers, 1990-91; Arizona Cardinals, 1991-93; St. Louis Rams, 1994; Tennessee Titans, 1995-96; Atlanta Falcons, 1997-2001; Chicago Bears, 2002-present
*Highlights:* Pro Bowl selection in 1997 and 1998…After 84 starts, he was among the top 35 rated passers in NFL history...took Atlanta to Super Bowl in 1999.

**Gary Clark, Wide Receiver**
*College:* James Madison
*Professional Career:* Jacksonville Bulls (USFL), 1984-85; Washington Redskins, 1985-92; Phoenix Cardinals, 1993-94; Miami Dolphins, 1995
*Highlights:* 699 career receptions…10,856 yards…Five seasons over 1,000 yards…Four-time Pro Bowl selection.

**Blanton Collier, Coach**
*College:* University of Kentucky
*Professional Career:* Cleveland Browns, 1963-70
*Highlights:* Followed the legendary coach Paul Brown…NFL career won-loss record of 76-34-2…Coached Browns to the NFL Championship in 1964.

**Glenn Dobbs, Coach**
*College:* Tulsa
*Highlights:* Consensus All-American as a player at Tulsa…Head coach, Tulsa, 1961-68…Longtime athletic director.

**John Elway, Quarterback**
*College:* Stanford University
*Professional Career:* Denver Broncos, 1983-98
*Highlights:* Three Super Bowl losses before winning Super Bowls XXXII and XXXIII…1987 NFL MVP…Four-time Pro Bowl selection…One of only 10 QBs in NFL history to throw for over 3,000 yards in 12 seasons…Second to Dan Marino in all-time total passing yards…No. 1 overall pick in 1983 draft.

**Brett Favre, Quarterback**
*College:* Southern Mississippi
*Professional Career:* Atlanta Falcons, 1991; Green Bay Packers 1992-present
Highlights: NFL MVP in 1995, '96 and '97…Five-time Pro Bowl selection…Threw 100 TD passes in 62 games, third fastest in NFL history…Led Packers to a Super Bowl victory in 1997.

**Doug Flutie, Quarterback**
*College:* Boston College
*Professional Career:* New Jersey Generals (USFL) 1984-85; Chicago Bears, 1986-87; New England Patriots, 1987-89; BC Lions (CFL) 1990-92; Calgary Stampeders (CFL), 1992-96; Toronto Argonauts (CFL) 1996-97; Buffalo Bills, 1998-2000; San Diego Chargers, 2001-present
*Highlights:* 1984 Heisman Trophy winner…Three-time Grey Cup MVP (CFL)…Six-time CFL Outstanding Player of the Year…First CFL quarterback to pass for more than 6,000 yards in a season.

**Dan Fouts, Quarterback**
*College:* University of Oregon
*Professional Career:* San Diego Chargers, 1973-87
*Highlights:* Pro Football Hall of Fame inductee...Third player ever to pass for more than 40,000 yards...Six-time Pro Bowl selection...Three-time All-Pro...NFL MVP in 1982...AFC Player of the Year 1979 and '82.

**Roman Gabriel, Quarterback**
*College:* North Carolina State
*Professional Career:* Los Angeles Rams, 1962-72; Philadelphia Eagles, 1973-77
*Highlights:* NFL MVP in 1969 when he recorded 24 TD passes versus only 7 INTs...Pro Bowl selection in 1968, '69, '72 and '74...1973 NFL Comeback Player of the Year.

**Otto Graham, Quarterback**
*College:* Northwestern
*Professional Career:* Cleveland Browns (AAFC), 1946-49; Cleveland Browns (NFL) 1950-55
*Highlights:* Pro Football Hall of Fame inductee...Guided Browns to 10 division or league titles in 10 years...Topped AAFC passers for four years, NFL passers for two years...All-League selection nine of 10 years...Threw 4 TD passes in 1951 NFL title game...Scored three TDs running and three passing in 1954 NFL title game.

**Jim Hanifan, Coach**
*College:* California
*Highlights:* Head coach, St. Louis Cardinals, 1980-85.

**Woody Hayes, Coach**
*College:* Denison
*Professional Career:* Coached three seasons at Denison, two at Miami of Ohio and 28 years as head coach at Ohio State.
*Highlights:* Five national championships at Ohio State... Buckeyes notched four unbeaten seasons and five seasons with just one loss... led his team to four consecutive Rose Bowls (1972 – 1975)... his lifetime record of 238 wins, 72 losses and 10 ties places him sixth all-time in NCAA Division I coaching victories.

**Leroy Kelly, Running Back**
*College:* Morgan State
*Professional Career:* Cleveland Browns, 1964-73
*Highlights:* Pro Football Hall of Fame inductee...Replaced Jim Brown in 1966...1,000-yard rusher in 1966, '67 and '68...Won NFL rushing titles in 1967 and '68...All-NFL 5 times...Six-time Pro Bowl selection.

**Dave Krieg, Quarterback**
*College:* Milton College
*Professional Career:* Seattle Seahawks, 1980-91; Kansas City Chiefs, 1992-93; Detroit Lions, 1994; Arizona Cardinals, 1995; Chicago Bears, 1996; Tennessee Titans, 1997-98
*Highlights:* Ranks eighth all-time in passing TDs...Ninth all-time in completions.

**Tom Landry, Head Coach**
*College:* University of Texas
*Highlights:* Pro Football Hall of Fame inductee...29 years as head coach of the Dallas Cowboys...Career record of 270-178-6...270 wins ranks third all-time...20 straight winning seasons...Five NFC titles...Two Super Bowl wins...Defensive back and punter with New York Yankees (AAFC) and New York Giants 1949-55.

**Steve Largent**
*College:* Tulsa
*Professional Career:* Played 14 years with the Seattle Seahawks.
*Highlights:* National Football Hall of Fame Inductee, 1995... elected into Oklahoma's 1st District Congressional seat in 1994. . . 1998 NFL Man of the Year for his commitment to community service... set six different career records and participated in seven Pro Bowls.

**Bobby Layne, Quarterback**
*College:* University of Texas
*Professional Career:* Chicago Bears, 1948; New York Bulldogs, 1949; Detroit Lions, 1950-58; Pittsburgh Steelers, 1958-62
*Highlights:* Led Lions to 4 divisional and 3 NFL titles in 1950s...Last-second TD pass won the 1953 NFL title game...All-NFL 1952 and 1956...NFL scoring champion, 1956...Career: 1,814 completions for 26,768 yards and 196 TDs...2,451 career rushing yards...Also kicked field goals...Scored 372 career points.

**Steve McNair, Quarterback**
*College:* Alcorn State
*Professional Career:* Houston Oilers/Tennessee Titans, 1995-present
*Highlights:* In first 87 games played: 2,288 attempts, 1,333 completions, 16,035 yards, passer rating of 81.3...In 2001 was second in the NFL in adjusted yards per pass.

**Peyton Manning, Quarterback**
*College:* Tennessee
*Professional Career:* Indianapolis Colts, 1998 to present
*Highlights:* Made his mark immediately...Set the following records in 1998: Most pass attempts as rookie, most pass completions as a rookie, most yards gained as a rookie, most TD passes as a rookie,

most consecutive games with a TD pass as a rookie...1999 Pro Bowl selection...1999 Second Team All-Pro...2000 Pro Bowl...No. 1 overall pick in 1998 draft.

**Don Meredith, Quarterback**
*College:* Southern Methodist
*Professional Career:* Dallas Cowboys, 1960-68
*Highlights:* Led Cowboys in passing from 1963 to 1968...Led Cowboys to their first winning season and the team's first NFL championship game in 1966...Two-time Pro Bowl selection...NFL Player of the Year in 1966...Enshrined in Cowboy Ring of Honor in 1976...One of the original voices of Monday Night Football.

**Art Monk, Wide Receiver**
*College:* Syracuse University
*Professional Career:* Washington Redskins, 1980-93; New York Jets, 1994; Philadelphia Eagles, 1995
*Highlights:* First-round draft pick...1980 NFL All-Rookie team...1985, '86 and '87 Pro Bowl selection...Nine 50-reception seasons, second only to Steve Largent...NFL's leading receiver of the 1980s with 662 catches...Career: 940 receptions for 12,721 yards and 68 TDs.

**Joe Montana, Quarterback**
*College:* Notre Dame
*Professional Career:* 1979 –1992 San Francisco 49ers; 1993-94 Kansas City Chiefs
*Highlights:* Master of come-from-behind victories. Led 49ers to four Super Bowl wins. Named Super Bowl MVP three times. Orchestrated 92-yard winning drive in closing seconds of Super Bowl XXIII. All-NFL three times, All-NFC five times. Missed entire 1991 season with injury. Selected to eight Pro Bowls. Career statis-

tics: 3,409 completions, 40,551 yards, 273 TDs, 92.3 passer rating.

**Warren Moon, Quarterback**
*College:* University of Washington
*Professional Career:* Edmonton Eskimos (CFL), 1978-83; Houston Oilers, 1984-93; Minnesota Vikings, 1994-96; Seattle Seahawks, 1997-98; Kansas City Chiefs, 1999-2000
*Highlights:* Canadian Football Hall of Fame inductee...Led Edmonton to 5 consecutive Grey Cup wins...Amassed 21,228 passing yards in CFL...In 1990 and 1991 led NFL in pass attempts...Led the NFL in completions in 1990, '91 and '95...In 1990 and '91 led the NFL in passing yards...In 1990 led the NFL in passing TDs...Ranks third all-time in attempts, completions and yards...1988 Pro Bowl MVP...Only Dan Marino and John Elway have thrown for more yards.

**Craig Morton, Quarterback**
*College:* California
*Professional Career:* Dallas Cowboys, 1965-74; New York Giants, 1974-76; Denver Broncos, 1977-82
*Highlights:* In first season with Broncos, led the team to its first-ever Super Bowl berth...His 1,929 yards, 14 TD passes, and team's 12-2 record earned him the AFC MVP and NFL Comeback Player of the Year awards...Member of the College Football Hall of Fame.

**Timm Rosenbach, Quarterback**
*College:* Washington State
*Professional Career:* Phoenix Cardinals, 1989-92, second player taken in the 1989 NFL Supplemental Draft; Hamilton TigerCats (CFL), 1994; New Orleans Saints, 1995. After two seasons as quarterbacks coach at Eastern Washington

University, Rosenbach joined his alma mater as quarterbacks coach in 2003.
*Highlights:* Set five single-season records as a Sophomore...Junior year, led WSU to its best season since 1930...a 9-3 campaign including a win over Houston in the Aloha Bowl...AP honorable mention All-America Team and a Davey O'Brien National Quarterback Award finalist...led NCAA Division I passers with a 160.7 Efficiency Rating...still holds Pac-10 records for total offense and yards per game passing.

**Mark Rypien, Quarterback**
*College:* Washington State
*Professional Career:* Washington Redskins, 1987-93; Cleveland Browns, 1994; St. Louis Rams, 1995; Philadelphia Eagles, 1996; St. Louis Rams, 1997; Indianapolis Colts, 2001.
*Highlights:* MVP in Super Bowl XXVI...Completed 18 of 33 passes for 292 yards and two TDs.

**Ricky Sanders, Wide Receiver**
*College:* Southwest Texas State
*Professional Career:* Washington Redskins, 1988-94; Atlanta Falcons, 1994
*Highlights:* Ranks fifth in Redskins history with 414 passes for 5,854 yards...Tied with Hugh Taylor, Charley Taylor, and Jerry Smith for most TD catches in a season (12) by a Redskins player...Set an NFL record 193 receiving yards and two TDs in Super Bowl XXII.

**Carl Smith, Coach**
*College:* Bakersfield College
*Professional Career:*
*Highlights:* Colorado 1972-73, Southwestern Louisiana 1974-78, Lamar 1979-1981, North Carolina State 1982. Philadelphia/Baltimore Stars (USFL) 1983-85, New Orleans Saints 1986-1996;

assistant head coach/quarterbacks coach, New England Patriots 1997; tight ends coach 1998 –99. Joined Cleveland Browns as quarterbacks coach in 2001.

**Bart Starr, Quarterback**
*College:* Alabama
*Professional Career:* Green Bay Packers, 1956-71
*Highlights:* Led Packers to 6 divisional titles, 5 NFL titles and 2 Super Bowl titles…NFL MVP in 1966…Super Bowl I MVP…Super Bowl II MVP…Three-time NFL passing champion…Four-time Pro Bowl selection.

**Roger Staubach, Quarterback**
*College:* Navy
*Professional Career:* Dallas Cowboys, 1969-79
*Highlights:* Heisman Trophy winner, 1963…Led Cowboys to 4 NFC titles and 2 Super Bowl wins (VI, XII)…MVP in Super Bowl VI…Four-time All-NFL selection…Four-time NFL passing leader.

**Joe Theismann, Quarterback**
*College:* Notre Dame
*Professional Career:* Washington Redskins, 1974-85
*Highlights:* Two-time Pro Bowl selection…Led Redskins to Super Bowl XVII victory over Miami Dolphins…1982 All-NFC…Lost to Oakland Raiders in Super Bowl XVIII…1983 All-NFL, AP NFL MVP, AP Offensive Player of the Year and Pro Bowl Player of the Game.

**Howard Twilley, Wide Receiver**
*College:* Tulsa
*Professional Career:* Miami Dolphins, 1966-76
*Highlights:* Member of the undefeated 1972 Miami Dolphins.

**Johnny Unitas, Quarterback**
*College:* Louisville
*Professional Career:* Baltimore Colts, 1956-72; San Diego Chargers, 1973
*Highlights:* Pro Football Hall of Fame inductee…Led Colts to 1958 and '59 NFL titles…All-NFL 5 times…MVP in 3 Pro Bowls…Threw at least one TD pass in 47 straight games…Had 26 games over 300 yards passing.

**Kurt Warner, Quarterback**
*College:* Northern Iowa
*Professional Career:* Iowa Barnstormers (Arena League), 1995-97; Amsterdam Admirals (NFL Europe), 1998, St. Louis Rams, 1998-present
*Highlights:* Emerged as an NFL star with an improbable year in 1999…1999 passer rating of 109.2 is fifth highest in NFL history…In 1999 led the NFL in TD passes, completion percentage, third down passer rating and fourth quarter passer rating…Set 8 Rams records…Threw more TD passes in first 4 NFL starts (14) than any QB in NFL history…Threw for more yardage in first 4 NFL starts than any QB in NFL history…Led Rams to first NFL title since 1951…Threw for a Super Bowl record 424 yards.

**Doug Williams, Quarterback**
*College:* Grambling
*Professional Career:* Tampa Bay Buccaneers, 1978-82; USFL, 1983-85; Washington Redskins, 1986-89
*Highlights:* Super Bowl XXII MVP…Completed 18 of 29 passes for 340 yards and 4 TDs, leading the Redskins to victory over the Denver Broncos.

**Jim Zorn, Quarterback**
*College:* Cal Poly-Pomona
*Professional Career:* Seattle Seahawks,

1976-84; Green Bay Packers, 1985; Tampa Bay Buccaneers, 1987

*Highlights:* 1976 NFC Offensive Rookie of the Year…Currently second behind Dave Krieg in Seahawks season records for completions, attempts and TD passes…Three consecutive 3,000-yard seasons…Only Seahawks QB to record back-to-back 300-plus yard games.

# About Jerry Rhome

### High School:
Quarterback
Dallas Sunset, Dallas, Texas
Byron Rhome, Head Coach (father)
Texas All State
All American
Voted Number 1 Player in the State of Texas 1959
Inducted into the High School Hall of Fame, Waco, Texas


### College:
Quarterback
University of Tulsa, Tulsa, Oklahoma
Glenn Dobbs, Head Coach
All American 1964
Heisman Trophy runner-up, 1964 (closest vote in history)
Walter Camp Trophy winner 1964
Associated Press Back of the Year 1964
Broke 18 NCAA Records in college
Oklahoma Sportsman of the Year 1964

Member of Oklahoma Sports Hall of Fame
Member of College Football Hall of Fame
Member of Texas High School Hall of Fame


### Pro Player:
Played quarterback for Dallas Cowboys,
Cleveland Browns, Houston Oilers, Los Angeles Rams

Played in three NFL Championship Games
Played in the Famous Ice Bowl Game December 31, 1967
in Green Bay


### Pro Coach:
Coached 24 Years in NFL:
Seattle Seahawks – QB Coach, wide receivers, Offensive Coordinator

Washington Redskins – QB Coach
San Diego Chargers – QB Coach and Offensive Coordinator
Dallas Cowboys – QB Coach
Arizona Cardinals – QB Coach, Offensive Coordinator
Minnesota Vikings – Wide Receivers Coach
Houston Oilers – QB Coach and Offensive Coordinator
St. Louis Rams – QB Coach and Offensive Coordinator
Atlanta Falcons – QB Coach

Coached in two Super Bowl Games:Winning in 1987–
Redskins 42/Broncos 0

## *Players Coached:*

| QB'S Played | Pro Bowl | Appeared in a SB |
|---|---|---|
| Jim Zorn (Seattle) | | |
| Dave Krieg (Seattle ) | Y | Y |
| Joe Theisman (Redskins) | Y | Y |
| Jay Schroeder (Redskins) | Y | |
| Doug Williams (Redskins) | Y | Y (MVP 1987) |
| Mark Rypien (Redskins) | Y | Y (MVP 1991) |
| Troy Aikman (Cowboys ) | Y | Y (MVP) |
| Chris Chandler (Arizona, Houston Oilers, Atlanta Falcons) | Y (Atl) | Y (Atl) |
| Steve Beurlein (Arizona Cards) | Y | Y |
| Warren Moon (Minnesota) | Y | |
| Steve McNair (Houston) | Y | Y |
| Kurt Warner (St. Louis) | Y | Y |

**Wide Receivers**

| | Pro Bowl | Appeared in a SB |
|---|---|---|
| Steve Largent (Seattle) | Y | Y |
| Chris Carter (Minnesota) | Y | |